Sprouts

Covenant Discipleship With Children

Edie Genung Harris

Shirley L. Ramsey

DISCIPLESHIP RESOURCES

PO BOX 340003 • NASHVILLE, TN 37203-0003
www.discipleshipresources.org

Cover design by Joey McNair

Book design by Sharon Anderson and Joey McNair

Edited by Linda R. Whited and David Whitworth

Library of Congress Control Number: 2002108150

ISBN 0-88177-389-1

DR389

Contents

PART 4: Leading Your Sprouts Group

PART 5: Worship Resources and Activity Ideas

PART 6: Resources for Additional Planning

➔ Permission is granted to reproduce resources marked with ➔ for use with a Sprouts program of a local church. Any other use requires permission from Discipleship Resources.

Part 1

Sprouts

What Is Sprouts?

Just as the branch cannot bear fruit by itself
unless it abides in the vine, neither
can you unless you abide in me.
John 15:4

Sprouts is a children's ministry for older elementary-school-age children who want to help one another grow in their faith in Jesus Christ. As part of their spiritual journey, they meet weekly to support one another and hold one another accountable to a group covenant that they have created and agreed upon. Sprouts is the children's version of the Covenant Discipleship groups supported by The United Methodist Church, which are based on John Wesley's class meetings.

Sprouts Is Unique

Sprouts is not Sunday school or a Bible study or a sharing group. It does not take the place of any Christian education program already in place in your church. Sprouts is a group setting where children can practice their discipleship. They *learn to do* the things they *learn about* in other settings.

Elementary-age children are primarily concrete thinkers. Sprouts translates "Love God and neighbor" and "What would Jesus do?" into specific acts so that they can understand and experience their discipleship. Sprouts provides a peer-group setting where children support and encourage one another in their Christian journey.

Because the adult leader of the Sprouts group is an active participant in keeping the group covenant, that adult forms a special relationship with the children that seldom occurs in any other church setting. The adult becomes both model and mentor of spiritual growth.

Parents, church leaders, and children themselves have testified to the difference that being in Sprouts has made in the lives of children. Children become more frequent and comfortable pray-ers. They read their Bibles more often. They feel closer to God. They are more generous, kinder, and more aware of and responsive to the needs of others. They become conscious of and concerned about justice issues such as homelessness or hunger. They translate their awareness and concern into action, finding ways to do something about it! Sprouts have sponsored recycling projects or educational/fundraising projects that impacted their local congregations in a life-changing way. Sprouts groups have often become the impetus for other discipleship groups in their churches, including inspiring adults to become involved in accountable relationships within their own Covenant Discipleship groups.

The Roots of Sprouts

While adults, teenagers, and folks in college have been participating in Covenant Discipleship (CD) groups since the 1970s,

"Sprouts is a positive force in a world filled with negative influences—a real help to parents."
—Parent of third- and fifth- grade Sprouts

"Before, I didn't come to church, and now I do."
—Mitch

"It has taught me how to get along with people better."
—Mick

"The most important thing is we are better people inside."
—Melanie

"The important thing about Sprouts is talking about situations that have happened to us...."
—Michael

"At first my mom talked me into it, then I loved it."
—Stephanie

"I read the Bible more and pray more."
—Taylor

"I made new friends—including Christ."
—Carly

"It helped me see that kids can help in many ways."
—Lyndi

it was not until 1994 that CD was adapted to fit the age-level requirements of older elementary-age children. Since teen groups are often called Branch groups, following Jesus' promise "I am the vine, you are the branches" (John 15:5), the children's version became known as Sprouts. Each Covenant Discipleship group agrees on a covenant based on the General Rule of Discipleship, a contemporary adaptation of John Wesley's General Rules, which relates directly to Jesus' Great Commandment:

> One of them, a lawyer, asked [Jesus] a question to test him. "Teacher, which commandment in the law is the greatest?" He said to him, " 'You shall love the Lord your God with all your heart, and with all your soul, and with all your mind.' This is the greatest and first commandment. And a second is like it: 'You shall love your neighbor as yourself.' On these two commandments hang all the law and the prophets."
>
> Matthew 22:35-40

Wesley knew that if we accept God's grace and steadfast love in our life, then we will want to respond to God's love by loving God and by loving our neighbor. Wesley methodically expressed Jesus' commandment in the General Rules, found in our *Book of Discipline* (¶ 103, pages 72-74).

Wesley stated that Christians will respond to God's commands "by doing no harm ..." "by ... doing good of every possible sort ..." and "by attending upon all the ordinances of God" (worship, ministry of the Word, Lord's Supper, prayer, studying Scripture, and fasting or abstinence).

The General Rule of Discipleship restates these General Rules: "To witness to Jesus Christ in the world, and to follow his teachings through acts of compassion, justice, worship, and devotion, under the guidance of the Holy Spirit."[1] Every group covenant contains clauses from each quadrant illustrated below, recognizing that we love God through Works of Piety (attending the ordinances of God), and we love our neighbor through Works of Mercy (doing good and not doing harm).

When they meet, group members give an account of how they have kept their covenant and how the Holy Spirit has been working in their lives.

A Sprout Is Not a Tree

Obviously, children have different needs, intellectual capabilities, spiritual formation issues, developmental levels, and social skills

Works of Mercy
(Loving Neighbors)

Acts of Compassion   Acts of Justice

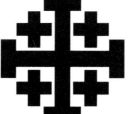

Acts of Devotion   Acts of Worship

Works of Piety
(Loving God)

For more information on the biblical, theological, and historical foundations of Covenant Discipleship, see the article on pages 32–34 and the list of related resources on page 92.

than adults or even teenagers. Sprouts resembles Covenant Discipleship for older folk in its form and substance, but there are differences in style and methodology.

Endnote

1 From *Guide for Covenant Discipleship Groups,* by Gayle Turner Watson (Discipleship Resources, 2000), page 12.

Ways Sprouts Is Like Covenant Discipleship for Adults and Teens

Membership is voluntary.
Groups meet weekly.
Each group creates its own covenant based on the General Rule of Discipleship.
Members report weekly on how they have kept the covenant.
Group members support one another.
Group members hold one another accountable.
Group members pray for one another.

Ways Sprouts Is Different From Covenant Discipleship for Adults and Teens

Covenant Discipleship	Sprouts
Adult language is used.	Works of Piety are Loving God. Works of Mercy are Loving Neighbors. Acts of Compassion are Acts of Kindness.
The meeting is one hour long.	The meeting is at least 90 minutes long.
There is little education on the meaning of worship, prayer, or other aspects of Christian living.	There are varying degrees of educational components based on needs of the particular group.
Although group members may sometimes agree to work together on a project, this would not substitute for the weekly meeting.	Education for and accomplishment of Acts of Justice are part of the Sprouts weekly meeting. Sometimes there are additional activities outside the weekly meeting.
Requires little preparation time to lead weekly sessions.	Requires an adult leader to plan, prepare, and lead weekly sessions.
Equal time and attention are given to all four Acts as long as members are successfully accomplishing them.	Varying degrees of emphasis and time are spent on each of the four Acts. The emphases are balanced over a longer course of time.
Journal keeping is encouraged, but optional.	Journal keeping is strongly encouraged, and each member is provided with a journal.
The method and content of Bible reading are up to each member.	Leaders provide varying degrees of structure and assistance in encouraging Bible reading.
Duration of the group is open-ended.	People join for a specific length of time, often corresponding to school semesters.

Part
2

Sprouts

Getting Your Sprouts Group Started

Go therefore and make disciples of all nations, ...teaching them to obey everything that I have commanded you.
Matthew 28:19-20

Choose a Sprouts Coordinator

The first step to take once you have decided to start a Sprouts group in your church is to select one person or a team of people to serve as the coordinator(s) for the ministry. If possible, choose people who are familiar with Covenant Discipleship. However, be assured that if no such person is available, any dedicated, interested person—lay, professional educator, or clergy—can implement the ministry.

Although it would be advantageous for the coordinator to have lots of extra time and energy to devote to this project, that will not be the case in most churches. This book, though, provides sufficient detail and explanation to help with the planning and coordination. The first duty of those interested in starting a Sprouts ministry will be to gather a team of willing workers to help carry out the task.

Once the Sprouts groups are underway, the coordinator's job will become easier as the leaders of the Sprouts group take on the task of planning. The coordinator's job at that point will be to plan for meeting with new parents and children who may want to join the Sprouts ministry, making sure that leaders have the supplies they need, and keeping the congregation informed about how the Sprouts program is contributing to the spiritual growth of their children.

Involve Church Leaders and Members

The first task of the Sprouts coordinator will be to seek support from the church leadership.

- Inform the pastor, the education ministry group, Council on Ministries, or other appropriate groups in your church about Sprouts. Solicit their assistance in interpreting the benefits of Covenant Discipleship with children.
- Distribute brochures that describe Sprouts (such as the sample on pages 17 and 18) to members of the congregation.
- Ask Sunday school teachers and other adult leaders with children to talk about Sprouts in their classes or groups.
- Display copies of the Sprouts poster (page 16) in places where every church member will have an opportunity to read about the program.
- Visit adult Sunday school classes to talk about Sprouts and to solicit support.

Identify Potential Participants

Sprouts can be used effectively with children in third, fourth, fifth, and sixth grades. The groupings you choose will be determined by the number, ages, and maturity of the children in your congregation and by the groupings of children in the schools in your area. Some possible groupings include:

- one group: for grades 3–6;
- two groups: one for grades 3–4 and one for grades 5–6;
- two groups: one for grades 3–5 and a separate group for grade 6;

- four groups: a separate group for each grade level;
- other options, depending on the needs of your congregation.

Remember: The conceptual thinking and skills required for a Covenant Discipleship group are beyond the developmental level of most first and second graders.

Once you have determined what groupings you will offer for Sprouts, invite children. You may want to include children who

- are from church families and already involved in your church programs: Sunday school, after-school programs, Scouts, vacation Bible school;
- attend special programs in your church but are not members of your church;
- are from families who are church members but are not active in the church currently;
- live in the neighborhood around your church;
- are friends and family members of children who attend your church.

Build Your Budget

Will your Sprouts activities be included in your church's budget for children's ministries or Christian education?

Will you be able to use the supplies that are purchased for Sunday school and other children's programs?

Are there resources already available in your church library, or will you need to purchase resource books and curriculum plans? (The resource list on pages 92–95 describes helpful resources for supporting a Sprouts ministry.)

Are there individuals who may be interested in providing financial assistance for a Sprouts group?

As you plan your budget for Sprouts, think about these items:

- publicity needs (printing, postage, and so forth)
- resources (books, videos, speakers' fees)
- leader training (photocopies, lunch, and so forth)
- refreshments
- supplies (for crafts, T-shirts, or other activities)

Decide When the Sprouts Group(s) Will Meet

Consider the schedules of the children you are inviting to participate in Sprouts groups. While you know that it is impossible to plan the perfect schedule for everyone, do the best you can. Here are some facts you will need to keep in mind:

- Each Sprouts meeting will last about ninety minutes;
- Each Sprouts term will last ten to twelve weeks.

Now, decide on which day of the week and at what time Sprouts will meet. Be sure to add these dates to your church's official calendar!

At the end of each term of Sprouts meetings, review the schedule. Are there changes that can be made that will make participation easier for the children? For their parents? For the leaders? Will a change in schedule make it possible for more children to participate? Don't hesitate to make adjustments when they are needed.

Decide Where the Sprouts Group(s) Will Meet

The size of your total group of Sprouts and the number of smaller Covenant Time groups (groups of no more than six children) within the total group will determine how many and what size rooms you will need. Each covenant group will need its own room for privacy. These rooms will need a table and chairs to provide a place for children to work on their journals.

Although each group will need its own private room for Covenant Time, several groups can meet together for Justice Time. If that will be your plan, reserve a room large enough for the total group. There you will need adequate space for children to move as they view videos, play simulation games, and/or do arts and crafts.

If you plan to serve refreshments during the Sprouts meetings, you will also need to consider the space needs for eating.

Recruit a Leadership Team

The number of leaders will be determined by the number of children who are participating in Sprouts. The Covenant Time groups should be limited to no more than six children each, and each Covenant Time group will need its own leader. However, several groups may come together for Justice Time with a single leader or team of leaders.

Unlike Covenant Discipleship groups for adults, Sprouts requires preparation time. As you choose your leadership team, look for caring, sensitive adults who will be strong role models and mentors. Consider inviting parents, Sunday school teachers, youth, professional staff, and/or anyone else interested in nurturing children through Covenant Discipleship to become part of your leadership team.

It is important that the leaders of Sprouts be people who are taking care of their own spiritual development as well as offering to lead children in spiritual formation. To be a good role model, a Sprouts leader should

- attend worship regularly;
- pray;
- read and study the Bible;
- give time and money to support the ministries of the church;
- be willing to participate as a full member of the Sprouts covenant group;
- participate in an adult Covenant Discipleship group, if possible;
- be genuinely concerned about the spiritual and emotional well-being of children.

If there is an adult Covenant Discipleship group in your congregation, that group may be a good place to start your search. If there is no adult Covenant Discipleship group in your church, perhaps your Sprouts leaders will be interested in starting an adult group after working with a few sessions of Sprouts.

Leadership team members serve as facilitators for the Covenant Time groups and leaders of the Justice Time.

- Since Covenant Time conversation is personal and confidential, the same leader(s) must be present each week. Do not, however, allow parents to be leaders of Covenant Time groups that include their own children.

- Leaders of the Justice Time, however, may change from week to week as the topics of discussion change. In addition to the regular leaders who will be present each week, consider inviting chairs of district and conference Church and Society work groups or mission work groups for special programs. You may also want to consider legislators, social workers, or urban ministry workers from time to time.

If transportation is an issue for some children, recruit leaders who will take the responsibility for bringing children to the meetings and/or taking them home. Since these people will spend time with the children, they also should be people who are knowledgeable about the Sprouts program and who are faithful Christians.

Suggestions for training leaders are found in Part 3 of this book, beginning on page 23.

Publicize Your Plans

Consider using some or all of these ideas as you plan ways to promote your Sprouts ministry:

- Send a flyer announcing Sprouts to all potential participants and their families. (See a sample on page 16.)

- Distribute brochures describing Sprouts to the congregation. (See the sample on pages 17–18.)

- Display flyers in store windows and/or put an article in your local newspaper if you have decided to invite the neighborhood children.

- Hold an informational meeting for parents and children. (See suggestions for this meeting on pages 14–15.)

- Enlist the support of your pastor and ask her or him to publicly support Sprouts.

- Ask Sunday school teachers and other adult leaders of children to talk about Sprouts in their classes or groups.

- Visit adult Sunday school classes and explain Sprouts to them.

- Talk with parents of potential Sprouts about how their children's spiritual formation will be enhanced through Sprouts.

- With all adults, emphasize the importance of the congregation in supporting children's faith formation. Ask for their support through prayer, financial assistance, and participation in leadership.

- Write articles for your church's newsletter, bulletin, or other publications. Once a Sprouts group has started in your church, you can invite the Sprouts to write such articles as well.

Plan an Informational Meeting

Invite the parents of children who are potential participants in Sprouts as well as key church leaders who will be involved in decisions about children's ministry to gather to learn more about the Sprouts program.

Send a letter to parents that describes something about what a Sprouts group is and how a child can benefit from participation in such a group.

You will find a sample letter to parents or guardians on page 19.

- Adapt the letter to make it appropriate for church members.

- Adapt the letter again for parents of children who are not active church participants. (Remember: Sometimes "church language" is difficult for those who are not actively involved.)

In each letter, talk about the partnership between church leaders and parents in nurturing children's faith. Enclose a brochure that describes the Sprouts program, a flyer about Sprouts, and a commitment form (see pages 16–20).

As You Plan the Meeting

- Decide if your meeting will be for parents and children or for parents only. If it is for parents only, be sure to plan another meeting to talk with children about Sprouts. You could even have the two meetings simultaneously, putting parents and children with different leaders.

- Arrange for a meeting room where participants will be comfortable.

- Make copies of any handouts you will use.

- Review the information that you will be presenting about Covenant Discipleship and Sprouts (see pages 32–34).

- Make preliminary decisions about meeting times and places for the Sprouts group.

- Provide for childcare during the meeting.

During the Meeting

- Give a brief overview of the General Rule of Discipleship and Covenant Discipleship groups. (Part 1 of this book and pages 32–34 about the historical, biblical, and theological foundations of Covenant Discipleship will provide the information you need. Make copies of pages 32–34 for the parents and leaders who attend.)

- Talk about examples of Works and Acts. (Have participants in the meeting refer to the Sprouts brochure they received in their invitation to the meeting as you speak. Have additional brochures available.)

- Explain what will happen in a typical Sprouts meeting. (Distribute copies of a sample covenant from page 66.) Remind the parents that the conversations in the Sprouts meetings are confidential.

- Talk about the partnership between parents and Sprouts leaders in the process of nurturing children's faith. Emphasize the importance of the parents' support and cooperation as they bring their children to the meetings each week and as they encourage their children to perform their Acts each week.

- Hand out a schedule for the upcoming term of Sprouts. Include the day of the week, the time, and the location for the meetings.

- Ask the children and parents to continue their discussion about participation in Sprouts at home and to pray about their involvement. Note that the decision to participate in Sprouts should be the child's, not the parent's. Sprouts requires a significant commitment, and children need to undertake it because they want to do it, not because of parental pressure.

- Provide a commitment form for each participant (sample on page 20). Note that the commitment form has two parts—a commitment by the child to participate and a commitment by the parents to support the child.

- Designate a date by which children and parents must return their signed commitment forms to the coordinator for Sprouts.

After the Informational Meeting

If there are parents/guardians who could not attend the informational meeting, call them to talk about what was explained and discussed in the informational meeting.

After the Sprouts Meetings Begin

A few weeks after the Sprouts program begins, contact the parents/guardians again to get feedback about how the Sprouts program is going for their children. Remind them about ways they can be helpful to their children. Emphasize that:

- regular attendance at Sprouts is important;

- the discussions between children and leaders at Sprouts meetings are confidential;

- the Sprouts leader is depending on responsible adults to encourage their children to perform works of Loving Neighbors and Loving God;

- the leaders are always available for parents/guardians or children.

Plan a Dedication Service

Include a dedication service for Sprouts children, leaders, and parents during a worship service prior to your first meeting of the term. Include a congregational commitment to support and nurture children's faith. (See page 21 for suggestions for this service.)

Sprouts

Witnessing for Jesus Christ
Through Loving God and Neighbor

WHO: For all 3rd–6th Graders who
- Want to be better Christians
- Want to know how to show love for God and other people
- Want to spend time with others who are growing in faith

WHAT: Just as a seed grows into a sprout and, finally, into a full-grown plant, in **SPROUTS** children have an opportunity to grow as Christian disciples. Participants learn to practice daily
- Acts of Kindness (helping others)
  - Acts of Justice (helping our world)
    - Acts of Devotion (relating to God)
      - Acts of Worship (praising God with others)

Weekly meetings include Covenant Time, a snack, and Justice Time.

WHEN: _____

WHERE: _____

SPROUTS
can help your faith grow!

Bring your parent(s) to an informational meeting on _____ at _____
                                                (date)   (time)

at _____
           (location)

You're sure to want to be a Sprout!

YES!

I am interested in Sprouts.

Name: _____

Grade: _____

Date: _____

Parent's Name: _____

Address: _____

_____

Phone: _____

Please Return to the Church Office.

A Sample Covenant

I want to love God and my neighbor. I want to witness to Jesus Christ in the world and to follow his teachings through **Acts of Kindness, Justice, Worship, and Devotion** under the guidance of the Holy Spirit. I promise these things to God, and I know that God will help me keep my promises and will forgive me when I make a mistake. I will be a faithful member of my group as we encourage and support one another.

- **I will worship each Sunday, if possible.**

- **I will pray each day.**

- **I will read my Bible.**

- **I will help someone every day.**

- **I will pick up after myself.**

- **I will make a poster about missions.**

- **I will write about my Acts in my journal and bring it to Sprouts each week.**

Sprouts

A Covenant Discipleship Group For Children

Witnessing for Jesus Christ Through Loving God and Neighbor

LOVING NEIGHBOR

Acts of Kindness
(helping others)
Sharing
Being nice to everyone
Giving money to a mission project

Acts of Justice
(helping our world)
Organizing a "Pick Up Litter Day"
Learning about UMCOR and
making a poster about it
Implementing a recycling program

• • • • •

LOVING GOD

Acts of Devotion
(relating to God)
Reading the Bible
Praying daily

Acts of Worship
(praising God with others)
Worshiping each week
Attending Sunday school

Planting the Seeds of Faith

John Wesley urged his followers to obey Jesus' commandment to love God and love your neighbor. Wesley explained how love should be shown in our actions by works of Loving Neighbor and Loving God. He believed that we should encourage and support one another In our efforts to be faithful disciples.

Since 1975, adults (Covenant Discipleship groups) and youth (Branch groups) have been meeting weekly for mutual accountability and support for Christian living. In January 1994, the first Sprouts group was started.

Sprouts provides Covenant Discipleship for older elementary-age children. Each Sprouts group writes a covenant in which they promise to witness to Jesus Christ in the world and follow his teaching through Acts of Kindness, Justice, Worship, and Devotion under the guidance of the Holy Spirit.

At each meeting, members
· share how they have lived out the covenant during the week;
· work together on a justice issue; and
· support each other in their efforts to **love God and neighbor.**

He also said, "With what can we compare the kingdom of God, or what parable will we use for it? It is like a mustard seed, which, when sown upon the ground, is the smallest of all the seeds on earth; yet when it is sown it grows up and becomes the greatest of all shrubs, and puts forth large branches, so that the birds of the air can make nests in its shade."
Mark 4:30-32

LOVING NEIGHBOR

KINDNESS   JUSTICE

DEVOTION   WORSHIP

LOVING GOD

Just as a seed grows into a sprout, and finally into a full-grown plant, in SPROUTS children have an opportunity to grow as disciples of Jesus Christ.

Dear _____ :

Your child is invited to participate in a special ministry called Sprouts. Based on the Covenant Discipleship ministry of The United Methodist Church, participants promise "to witness to Jesus Christ in the world and to follow his teachings through Acts of Kindness, Justice, Worship, and Devotion, under the guidance of the Holy Spirit." Group members develop skills in supporting one another in their efforts to be disciples of Jesus Christ. This will be a growing and learning experience that will impact the children as they learn how to better live out their desire to love God and their neighbors.

Enclosed you will find a brochure and a flyer with the date, time, and location of Sprouts meetings. We will also be having a parent/guardian meeting to provide information about this significant opportunity for your child to grow in faith and discipleship. This meeting will be held on _____ at _____ in _____ .
　　　　　　　　　　　　　　(date)　　　　　　　(time)　　　　　　　(location)
If you are unable to attend this meeting, we will be happy to discuss Sprouts with you at your convenience.

Each Sprouts group (4-6 children with an adult facilitator) writes a covenant intended to help participants follow Jesus' command to his disciples, "Love the Lord your God with all your heart, and with all your soul, and with all your mind, and with all your strength . . . [and] love your neighbor as yourself." During weekly Sprouts meetings, the children and their adult facilitator discuss how well they have lived up to their covenant during the preceding week. Group members also explore issues of justice, such as hunger, the environment, or peace.

One of the main emphases in Sprouts is self-discipline and self-motivation. The group provides confidentiality, mutual support, and accountability for Christian discipleship. However, we hope that you will support your child's attendance each week and her or his efforts to grow in Loving God and Loving Neighbor. Also, please make sure your child has a quiet setting appropriate for Bible study and personal prayer as well as an opportunity to take part in family prayer and devotions. If your child decides to participate, please complete the enclosed Commitment to Participation form and hand it in at the informational meeting or return it to the church office.

We hope your child will want to be a part of Sprouts! We believe it can be an important step in his or her faith journey.

Peace and Joy,

The Sprouts Leaders

Sprouts Commitment to Participation

After you have discussed your participation in **Sprouts** with your parent(s) or guardian(s), both you and your parent will sign the Commitment to Participation below. Return the form to _____ by _____.

date

I want to witness to **Jesus Christ** in the world and to follow his teachings through

Acts of Kindness, Justice, Worship, and **Devotion.**

Under the guidance of the Holy Spirit and with the support of my group members, I will participate in **Sprouts**.

_____   _____
Sprout's Signature   *Date*

I will support _____ as a
participant in Sprouts.   *(name of child)*

_____   _____
Parent/Guardian Signature   *Date*

Cut here and keep the information below as a reminder.

+ +

Sprouts will meet on _____ at _____
                                    (day of week)   *(time)*
        from_____ to_____ .
            (beginning date)   *(ending date)*

I want to witness to **Jesus Christ** in the world and to follow his teachings through

Acts of Kindness, Justice, Worship, and **Devotion.**

Under the guidance of the Holy Spirit and with the support of my group members, I will participate in **Sprouts**.

_____   _____
Sprout's Signature   *Date*

I will support _____ as a
participant in Sprouts.   *(name of child)*

_____   _____
Parent/Guardian Signature   *Date*

Litany of Dedication for Sprouts and Sprouts Leaders

Pastor: In baptism we are born anew by water and the Spirit and called to be faithful disciples of Jesus Christ. This calling is for all ages and for all who seek God's reign of justice and love. Children, no less than adults, are empowered to live as faithful members and are God's representatives in the world.

Sprouts Leader: We present today these children to be members of a Sprouts group. They are growing in their faith. They are learning how to be disciples together by watching over each other in love.

Children: Jesus calls us to love God with all our hearts and minds and souls and strength, and to love our neighbors. As Jesus' disciples, he calls us to witness to him in the world and to follow his teachings.

Parents (with hands on the shoulders of their children): By God's grace, we will support our children in all their efforts to live and grow as Christian disciples. We promise them our loving care, counsel, and faithful example.

Children: By the Spirit's power given in baptism,* we will perform Acts of Kindness, Acts of Justice, Acts of Worship, and Acts of Devotion. We welcome God working these acts through us. We will be faithful Sprouts.

Sprouts Leaders: Rooted in faith, we undertake this venture. We are confident that Sprouts is a faithful practice of mutual support for accountability and growing in God's grace.

Congregation: We reaffirm the vow we make at every baptism. We will surround them with a community of love and forgiveness so that they may grow in their trust of God and be found faithful in their service to others. We will pray for them that they may be true disciples who walk the way that leads to life.

Pastor: May we all remember God's promise to be with us. May we know God's presence with us as we make this covenant to be God's disciples and to follow the teaching of Jesus Christ under the guidance of the Holy Spirit. Amen.

---

* United Methodists affirm the universal work of the Holy Spirit in the lives of all people, including Sprouts children who have not yet been baptized (prevenient grace). In baptism, with the laying on of hands, United Methodists affirm the special work of the Spirit in the lives of those who are baptized.

Part 3

Sprouts

Training Your Leaders

Speaking the truth in love, we must grow up in every way into him who is the head, into Christ.
Ephesians 4:15

Schedule a Training Session

Before your leaders begin meeting with Sprouts groups, plan for one or more training meetings of all leaders. If nearby churches are also planning Sprouts, a joint leader-training session might be a good idea since you will have a larger number of leaders together than you will recruit within your own church. In fact, you may want to plan a district event that is both a training session for leaders who will be leading Sprouts and a promotional meeting. The promotional aspect of the meeting would get the word out to other churches about what can happen among their children if they choose to use the Sprouts program.

Depending on the number of leaders you will be training, you will want to plan for a training event of a few hours or for a whole day. Here is a sample schedule for an all-day event. Use this schedule or adapt it to fit the needs of the meeting you are planning.

One-Day Training Session for Leaders of Sprouts

8:30–9:00	Refreshments/Get Acquainted
9:00–9:15	Worship
9:15–10:00	Learn About Covenant Discipleship With Children
10:00–10:45	Learn About Older Elementary-Age Children
10:45–11:00	Break
11:00–11:45	Learn About Covenant Time and the Responsibilities of Covenant Time Leaders
11:45–12:30	Lunch
12:30–1:15	Learn About Justice Time and the Responsibilities of Justice Time Leaders
1:15–1:45	Talk About What Sprouts Leaders Must Be and Do
1:45–2:00	Break
2:00–2:30	Use the Sprouts Book and the Session-Planning Helps to Begin Plans for the First Sprouts Meeting
2:30–3:00	Evaluate and Close

Plan What Leaders Need to Know

Be sure that each leader has a copy of this book, *Sprouts: Covenant Discipleship With Children*. Encourage them to read the entire book so that they will know how to use it in their planning for Sprouts sessions.

During the training session you will want to include conversation and activities about a variety of topics. The information you will need is printed in "What Is Sprouts?" (Part 1), here in Part 3, and in "Leading Your Sprouts Group" (Part 4). Be sure that you talk about:

- what a Sprouts program can offer the children in your congregation, including how it is different from Sunday school (page 6);
- the historical, biblical, and theological background of Covenant Discipleship (pages 32–34);
- information about the age-level characteristics of the children who will be in their groups (page 48);
- the content and format of a Sprouts meeting, including its division into Covenant Time and Justice Time (pages 30–31, 52–62, and 65);
- discussion of language issues for children, including knowing the difference between kindness and justice (pages 44–45 and 49);
- responsibilities of Covenant Time leaders (pages 28–29);
- responsibilities of Justice Time leaders (pages 29–30);
- the aids included in this book that can help them understand Sprouts and help them plan for meaningful meetings;
- the importance of personal practice of spiritual disciplines: prayer, Bible study, worship, Christian conversation, the sacraments, fasting.

On the next few pages there are suggestions for activities that you may choose to use in your training session. There are several ways to use these suggestions:

- The Covenant Discipleship or Justice Time areas might be most appropriate for an educational or promotional event.
- A full-day event might use one or more activities from each area.
- Each content area might be material for an individual session.
- Some of the components may also be used as ongoing training.
- At the least, the adults involved in Sprouts should read through the various experiences and respond mentally or in writing in order to prepare themselves for leadership.

Many of the issues in these content areas overlap, so some of the experiences in the different sections may seem somewhat repetitive. Select one or more activities in each content area that are most suitable for your group of leaders and make the best use of your time and space.

Learn About Covenant Discipleship With Children

The Sprouts Coordinator must be familiar with Covenant Discipleship development, history, and theory. The "Resources for Additional Planning" section, which begins on page 91, lists helpful books and other materials. Churches that have participated in adult Covenant Discipleship groups or Branch groups for youth may also be a source of books or videos. For your leader training session, select from the following activities:

- Look up Scripture references to covenants: Genesis 9:8-17 (Noah); Genesis 17 (Abraham); Exodus 19:3-6 (Moses); Deuteronomy 6:1-9 (the Shema); Jeremiah 31:31-34; Hebrews 8:6-13 (the new covenant). Discuss the meaning of these covenants for today. Discuss the difference between a contract and a covenant.

- Read Matthew 22:36-40 and Mark 12:28-31 ("The Great Commandment"). Brainstorm ways we can love God and ways we can love our neighbor. List your ideas on a chalkboard or sheet of newsprint. Discuss how Jesus' command relates to the Old Testament covenants.

- Read "The Nature, Design, and General Rules of Our United Societies" on pages 72–74 in *The Book of Discipline of The United Methodist Church, 2000.* John Wesley, as part of his General Rules, lists behaviors that are encouraged, as well as behaviors that are not acceptable for Christians. Notice how these relate to loving God and loving neighbors. Discuss which of Wesley's rules are pertinent today.

- Present a brief overview of Works of Mercy/Loving Neighbors (Acts of Compassion/Kindness and Justice) and Works of Piety/Loving God (Acts of Worship and Devotion). Use *Accountable Discipleship: Living in God's Household,* pages 24–29, as a guide for your discussion. You will find an illustration of the concept on page 35. Ask the participants to speak in pairs to discuss their thoughts about balancing public and private acts of Christian discipleship.

- Begin a journal. Ask the leaders to write in a notebook or on a sheet of paper: (1) what they are now doing on a regular basis to love God and neighbor, and (2) what they would be willing to begin doing to love God and neighbor.

- Recruit someone who has been in a Covenant Discipleship group to talk about how Covenant Discipleship influenced his or her life. If there are children in your area who have participated in Sprouts, invite one or more of them to tell about their experiences. Ask several people who have been involved in Covenant Discipleship to role-play a meeting.

- Review the historical, biblical, and theological foundations of Covenant Discipleship (pages 32–34). Provide copies for leaders who may want to read and review this information later.

Learn About Older Elementary-Age Children

As you prepare to lead this section of the leader training, check the books in the resource list on pages 92–95 for help.

From the following activities choose those that best meet the needs of your leaders.

- Ask each leader to think of an older elementary-age child she or he knows. Then have each leader write down as many characteristics of the child as possible in three to four minutes. As a group, make a composite list of all the characteristics. Your list might include:

Active *Growing independence*
Imaginative *Learning to think abstractly*
Talkative *Curious*
Enjoys reading aloud *Peer-group-centered*

- Think about the things you want the children in your congregation to know, understand, and experience about God, Jesus, the Bible, and the church. Make a list for each category on a piece of newsprint or on a chalkboard. Compare these lists with your list of age-level characteristics. Talk about how you can plan effectively for meaningful participation that leads to faith and discipleship, while keeping in mind children's individual needs and characteristics.

- Recruit a schoolteacher, counselor, church educator, or other "expert" to speak to your group concerning children's developmental levels and appropriate methods for teaching and facilitating learning.

- If you have children with special needs (learning disabilities, physical disabilities, and so forth), invite a special-education teacher to make a presentation about including these children in your group.

- Create a slide show with photographs of older elementary-age children in Sunday school, at the mall, at a ball game, or other settings children of this age group enjoy.

- Have each leader interview an older elementary-age child about what she or he enjoys doing, favorite TV shows or movies, concerns about the world in which we live, and questions about God.

- Most older elementary-age children still think concretely. Set up several learning activities appropriate for this age group to illustrate ways to help children understand abstract theological concepts. For example, to help children understand Acts of Compassion (Kindness), you might focus on the story of the good Samaritan (Luke 10:25-37). Activities could include:
  - completing a crossword puzzle that reinforces learning the story;
  - learning the song "The Good Samaritan," by Mary Lu Walker;
  - creating get-well cards for congregational members who are in the hospital;
  - writing a prayer of confession for times we have not responded to the needs of others.

After leaders have had an opportunity to explore the various learning activities, point out that children learn in a variety of ways. Activities and questions should also match the varied levels of maturity of your children.

- Discuss the difference between teaching and leading a group. How do the leaders see their role as facilitators? How can they help the children assume leadership within the group?

- Distribute copies of "Children and Justice: Age-Level Characteristics" from page 48. Talk about how accurately these descriptions match the children the leaders know will be in their Sprouts groups.

Learn About Covenant Time

Covenant Time will be approximately forty-five minutes of each week's Sprouts session. The discussions and activities of Covenant Time will focus on the elements of the unique covenant that each group will make for itself during the first few weeks that it meets. As you train leaders to lead Covenant Time, you may be able to use some of these suggested activities.

- Post sample covenants on a bulletin board or wall. Use covenants from previous Sprouts groups or use the sample covenant on page 66 of this book.

- Discuss the role of the group covenant as the statement of the group's commitment to be involved in Acts of Kindness, Justice, Worship, and Devotion.

- Discuss realistic levels of commitment for your group. Remember that children can overextend themselves when they get excited. If you know which children will be in your group, consider their outside activities, parental support, and levels of maturity. Work on a strategy for helping children set realistic goals for themselves.

- Brainstorm possibilities for the Acts of Worship and Acts of Devotion sections of the covenant.

- Role-play creating a covenant in a Covenant Time group. (Concentrate on the Acts of Worship and Acts of Devotion first. Plan to add Acts of Kindness and Acts of Justice after talking about Justice Time.)

- Review the suggested outline for the first Sprouts meeting, pages 52–54. Concentrate on the part of the outline related to Covenant Time (pages 52–53). What special needs or concerns do you see in your group? Discuss how you might adapt this outline to fit your children and your unique situation.

- Give each leader a piece of clay. Ask the leaders to create a sculpture that symbolizes what they think it will feel like to be a part of a Covenant Time group with children. If you have a small group, let each leader tell about her or his sculpture with the total group. If you have a large group of leaders, ask the group members to talk about their sculptures in pairs.

- Make a list of questions or issues that older elementary-age children might be concerned about or to which it might be difficult to respond (for example, "Why doesn't God answer my prayers?"). Talk about appropriate ways to respond to these questions. Don't be afraid to say that you do not know an answer. You may sometimes need to respond, "That's a good question. It is hard to understand. I have a problem with that one too." Emphasize that the point is not to find correct answers but to feel comfortable discussing complex issues with children. Identify possible resources and resource people who can provide help with these discussions.

- Play a matching game. On sheets of construction paper, print the words or phrases from columns 1 and 2, one word or phrase per sheet.

Column 1	Column 2
Savior	Jesus
Holy Spirit	feeling God with us
Kingdom of God	the world as God wants it to be
Discipleship	
Watching Over One Another in Love	learning to follow Jesus
	caring about how group members are learning to follow Jesus

Mount the words or phrases from Column 1 on a bulletin board or easel. Mount the words or phrases from Column 2 in random order nearby. Ask leaders to match each of the scattered words or phrases with the word or phrase from Column 1 that it describes or defines. If time permits, let leaders write their own definitions for the first set of words or phrases or add other words with definitions appropriate for older elementary-age children. Use the game to stimulate discussion of helping children understand and develop their own theological language.

- Recruit someone who has been in an adult Covenant Discipleship group or who has led Covenant Time in a Sprouts group to speak about the covenant and its possible impact on the children.

Learn About Justice Time

In addition to Covenant Time, each Sprouts session includes Justice Time. During Justice Time, Sprouts children learn about and practice Acts of Kindness and Acts of Justice.

Covenant Discipleship deliberately makes a distinction between Acts of Compassion or Kindness and Acts of Justice. The distinction is sometimes hard for children to understand and implement, just as it is for adults. You may want to include one or more of the following learning experiences to prepare leaders for leading Justice Time.

- Divide leaders into smaller groups of four or five. Give each group a copy of "Justice: Understanding, Implementing It," from pages 42–43. Ask each group to read the article and discuss what the article says to them about being Sprouts leaders. After ten to fifteen minutes, call the groups together to report on their findings.

- Explore Scripture passages that emphasize justice as an essential component of loving God and neighbor. (Hint: Check your Bible concordance for justice issues, such as hunger, treatment of prisoners, or the poor.)

- Use "What's the Difference Between Kindness and Justice?" (page 49) to help the leaders create their own lists of examples that illustrate the difference between Acts of Kindness and Acts of Justice.

- Give each leader a sheet of paper and a crayon or marker. Instruct the leaders to fold their paper into thirds. On one third let them draw an Act of Kindness or Justice that a group within your church is doing. On another third of the paper, have them draw an Act of Justice or Kindness that an individual in your church is doing. On the final third, have them draw an Act of Kindness or Justice that they are doing.

- Choose a justice subject, such as hunger, homelessness, or interracial relations. List Acts of Kindness and Acts of Justice that children could do individually or as a group.

- Discuss why individuals and churches are more likely to do Acts of Kindness than Acts of Justice.

- Recruit a district or conference "expert" on social justice issues to talk about the kindness/justice differentiation, to suggest justice or kindness activities, to recommend resources, and/or to tell about justice ministries that are operating in your area.

- Have the leaders role-play the completion of the group covenant they began when they talked about creating a group covenant during the Covenant Time activities. (See the Justice Time section of the suggested outline for the first Sprouts meeting, on page 54.)

- Provide a resource table display. Allow time for leaders to review the resources. Have them choose a justice topic they want to include in Justice Time in their own Sprouts groups.

Plan the First Sprouts Meeting

Be sure that you allow some time during your training session for leaders to begin planning for their first Sprouts meeting. Give each one a copy of the "Sprouts Session-Planning Sheet" (page 65) and "Plan Your First Sprouts Meeting" (pages 52–54). Let the leaders work in groups to begin their plans for a first session.

As the leaders plan a first session, remind them that they will want to:

- review their own understandings about Sprouts and be prepared to answer any questions the children may have;

- think about how they will insure that the children will be able to talk freely and confidentially about important issues;

- brainstorm possible Acts the children might be willing to perform as part of their covenant;

- remember that it may take two or three weeks for explanations and for creating a group covenant, especially with a group of new Sprouts;

- decide how they will be sure that each child has a Bible at home;

- determine how they will help children know how to use their Bibles: using reading assignments during the week, for instance, and assignments to evaluate and develop Bible-use skills.

Assign Children and Leaders to Sprouts Groups

Once you have children registered for Sprouts and you have trained the adult leaders, you are ready to assign children and leaders to Sprouts groups. As you make assignments, keep these guidelines in mind:

Covenant Groups
- Covenant Time groups may be mixed-grade or single-grade groups, depending on what works best for the children in your groups.
- There should be no more than six children in a Covenant Time group.
- Each Covenant Time group needs one adult facilitator who can be present regularly.
- The discussions that take place in a Covenant Time group are confidential and must not be discussed by the children or the leaders outside that setting (with the exception of concerns about the possibility of abuse or other harm that may come to a child).
- Remember that children younger than third grade will probably have difficulty with the concepts and skills required for a Covenant Discipleship group.

Justice Groups
- Several Covenant Time groups can meet together for Justice Time.
- Provide a sufficient number of adult leaders to plan and carry out the Justice Time projects. These leaders may be the same ones each week or may change from week to week.
- Look for ways to help the children choose their own justice issues for Justice Time. (See the helps on pages 62–63.)
- Outside speakers and leaders (such as missions chairpersons or directors of community service projects) may be a valuable addition to Justice Time.
- Remember that younger children may have difficulty distinguishing between kindness and justice and may require additional help.

Get Ready for the Dedication Service

Show the leaders the "Litany of Dedication for Sprouts and Sprouts Leaders" on page 21.

Provide time for the leaders to talk about the responsibility that will be theirs as they provide adult leadership for the spiritual formation of children.

Conclude the training session in prayer for the adults who will lead and for the children who will be guided by their participation with these leaders in Sprouts groups.

Foundations for Covenant Discipleship Groups

Historical Foundation

Covenant Discipleship groups and Sprouts have their roots in the Methodist class meetings of the early Methodist movement. In 1739 John Wesley began preaching in the open air to ordinary people who seldom attended church. He preached in fields and town squares to factory workers, miners, mill workers, carpenters, shop keepers, and teachers. Many of those people responded to Wesley's preaching and were led to experience repentance and forgiveness for their sins. They were encouraged by Wesley to meet with others who had formed a local religious society. These societies were gatherings of men and women who shared a common experience of faith in God. They provided the support people needed in order to learn about and grow in their relationship with Christ.

Later in 1739 two societies in Bristol, England, joined together, with Wesley's help, to purchase some land and build a new meeting house. This building was known as the "New Room." By 1742, Wesley was finding it difficult to pay the mortgage each month. At a meeting one night a group of society leaders and Wesley came up with a plan to pay off the debt. Wesley would divide the society into smaller groups, called classes, according to where people lived. He then appointed a responsible leader to each class. The leader's job was to visit each person in his class once a week to collect a penny. If the person could not afford to give the penny, the leader would give it for them. At the end of the month the leaders would meet with Wesley to turn in the money. In this way the members of the society would be able to retire the debt on the New Room.

They soon discovered that having the leaders visit door-to-door each week was an effective way of keeping in touch with and caring for people. Eventually the people began to meet together as a group with their leader once a week.

The class meeting was a weekly time of prayer, hymn-singing, Bible study, and accountability. It was in the class meeting that many Methodists learned Christian faith and that they received the support they needed to live it out in their daily lives.

The rule of life for the Methodist societies and classes was Wesley's General Rules. The General Rules provided directions for their life together and in the world as followers of Jesus Christ. The purpose of this Methodist rule of life was to help the people be faithful to the commands of Jesus to love God with all their hearts, souls, minds, and strength and to love their neighbor as themselves (Luke 10:25-37). There are three rules, or guides, for Methodist life together:

First: Do no harm, by avoiding evil of every kind, especially that which is most generally practiced. . . .
Second: Do good of every possible sort, and, as far as possible, to all people.
Third: Attend upon all the ordinances of God:
- The public worship of God;
- Ministry of the Word;
- The Lord's Supper;
- Family and private prayer;
- Reading and studying the Bible;
- Fasting or abstinence.

The General Rules are simple. John Wesley's original version is found in ¶ 103 of *The Book of Discipline of The United Methodist Church—2000* (pages 72-74).

Covenant Discipleship groups and Sprouts are a contemporary adaptation of the Methodist class meeting. The General Rule of Discipleship—to witness to Jesus Christ in the world and to follow his teachings through Acts of Compassion, Justice, Worship, and Devotion under the guidance of the Holy Spirit—is a summary of the General Rules used by the societies and classes. These General Rules help Sprouts learn about following Jesus Christ in their world just as the General Rules and class meetings helped Methodist boys and girls, women and men for more than 150 years.

Biblical Foundation

The parable of the good Samaritan (Luke 10:25-37) is a good place to begin building a biblical foundation for Sprouts. It is a story through which Jesus gives us a clear picture of the demands of following him. In it we see that following Jesus involves living a life balanced between faith and caring; between being and doing.

In this parable we see that following Jesus is a way of life grounded in a relationship with him. This is a relationship of unconditional love, forgiveness, and acceptance from God for human beings. Our part in the relationship is to love God with all our heart, with all our soul, with all our strength, and with all our mind. The way we live out God's love is by loving our neighbor as ourselves. The story Jesus tells about the good Samaritan teaches us that our neighbor is anyone, anywhere in the world, who is suffering and in need of compassion and justice.

In other words, "We know love by this, that he laid down his life for us—and we ought to lay down our lives for one another. How does God's love abide in anyone who has the world's goods and sees a brother or sister in need and yet refuses help? Little children, let us love, not in word or speech, but in truth and action" (1 John 3:16-18). Following Jesus is a way of life that is defined by self-giving, unconditional love. This is a love that must be learned. It is learned by spending time with Jesus and with other sisters and brothers, teachers, mentors, and friends who have given their lives to Jesus and who have spent years learning and practicing his life.

Jesus said, "I am the vine, you are the branches. Those who abide in me and I in them bear much fruit, because apart from me you can do nothing" (John 15:5). We cannot follow and live with Jesus alone. Life with Jesus is life lived in community. We live and learn to follow Jesus together with others, in community. The community of Jesus draws us to him and keeps us with him through its life, worship, and teaching. The community of Jesus is like a grapevine. Jesus is the vine that is the source of life and nourishment for the branches. The sprouts from the vine grow into branches that are intertwined and interdependent with one another. They grow together and work together to bear fruit that gives life to the vine and to the world. The fruit of this vine is love.

The love Jesus gives and shares with those who come to him and follow him is revealed to the world in Acts of Kindness and Justice. This love is nurtured through Acts of Worship and Devotion.

In Sprouts, children gather together to learn Jesus' life and love from faithful adults who walk with Jesus. Their faith is nurtured and helped to grow as they learn and practice the basics of Christian faith: compassion, justice, worship, and devotion.

Theological Foundation

Sprouts is firmly rooted in the Wesleyan way of salvation. Mutual accountability and support for Christian discipleship has deep roots in the theology of John Wesley and the people called Methodists. The place most early Methodists learned their theology was in the hymns of Charles Wesley. Many of his hymns were poetic summaries of the way of salvation. Look at the example below:

Love Divine, All Loves Excelling

1. Love divine, all loves excelling,
   Joy of heaven, to earth come down,
   Fix in us thy humble dwelling;
   All thy faithful mercies crown!
   Jesus, thou art all compassion,
   Pure, unbounded love thou art;
   Visit us with thy salvation!
   Enter every trembling heart.

2. Come, almighty to deliver,
   Let us all thy grace receive;
   Suddenly return, and never,
   Never more thy temples leave.
   Thee we would be always blessing,
   Serve thee as thy hosts above,
   Pray, and praise thee without ceasing,
   Glory in thy perfect love.

3. Finish then thy new creation,
   Pure and spotless let us be;
   Let us see thy great salvation
   Perfectly restored in thee;
   Changed from glory into glory,
   Till in heaven we take our place,
   Till we cast our crowns before thee,
   Lost in wonder, love, and praise.

Jesus is God's love come to the world as a human being. He makes the first move and helps us to open our eyes, minds, and hearts to his love for us. Jesus wants to make his home in our hearts. He wants to live in and with us. Our part is to invite him and let him in.

When we accept God's acceptance of us and let Jesus into our hearts, he begins the work of changing our lives. He begins by letting us know that our sins are forgiven, we are loved unconditionally by God, and God has adopted us as God's own daughters and sons. When Jesus is at home in us, we are at home with God. Our response to this new relationship is prayer, praise, and service. We pray and praise so that we always remember who and whose we are: that we are children of God living in God's household.

As we live together in God's household and follow the household rules (loving God with all that we are and all that we have and loving our neighbor as ourselves), love transforms our character. Love heals and restores and makes us whole. As we allow it, through loving God and loving all that God loves, grace works in, with, and for us and makes each of us into the person God created us to be. The goal of life in God's household is to make each of us complete and whole human beings, just like Jesus.

Sprouts helps children and adults learn and live this faith and accept God's good news for themselves. It helps them to practice and grow in faith by practicing the basics, by doing the things that Jesus taught his disciples to do. They learn about living in God's household as a child of God who is forgiven, loved, and free to become the person God created her or him to be. In the process, as they learn and grow in faith, hope, and love, others see and experience the love of God through, with, and in them. That is what salvation is all about. That is what Christian life is all about. That is what Sprouts is all about.

_____

To learn more about John Wesley and the Methodists, see:

Accountable Discipleship: Living in God's Household, by Steven W. Manskar (Discipleship Resources, 2000).

A Real Christian: The Life of John Wesley, by Kenneth J. Collins (Abingdon Press, 1999).

Wesley and the People Called Methodists, by Richard P. Heitzenrater (Abingdon Press, 1995).

To learn more about the theological foundations of Sprouts, see:

Accountable Discipleship: Living in God's Household, by Steven W. Manskar (Discipleship Resources, 2000).

The New Creation: John Wesley's Theology Today, by Theodore Runyon (Abingdon Press, 1998).

The Scripture Way of Salvation: The Heart of John Wesley's Theology, by Kenneth J. Collins (Abingdon Press, 1997).

LOVING NEIGHBORS

ACTS OF KINDNESS

*Whoever pursues righteousness
and kindness
will find life and honor.*
(Proverbs 21:21)

Give money to a mission project
Write or call a grandparent
Be a friend to a new student at school
Help a family member or teacher
Invite a friend to Sunday school
Do a chore without being asked
Give money to a homeless shelter

ACTS OF JUSTICE

*When justice is done, it is a joy to
the righteous.*
(Proverbs 21:15)

Do a project for a homeless shelter
Organize a recycling project
Participate in a United Methodist mission project, the Heifer Project, or Habitat for Humanity
Write letters to members of Congress
Support daycare/Head Start

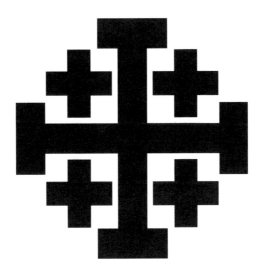

ACTS OF DEVOTION

*How can young people keep their way pure?
By guarding it according to your word.*
(Psalm 119:9)

Read your Bible
Pray
Read a book about a character in the Bible or a well-known modern-day Christian
Learn about the Christian year
Sing praises to God
Keep a journal

ACTS OF WORSHIP

*I was glad when they said to me,
"Let us go to the house of the LORD!"*
(Psalm 122:1)

Attend a worship service
Attend Sunday school
Be an acolyte
Sing in the choir
Tithe (give money regularly to the church)
Receive the Lord's Supper

LOVING GOD

Don't Assume . . .

. . . that there is a significant difference between churched and unchurched kids or their parents.

- Even families who are long-time church members might not have the background you would expect.

- Some will have come from other faith traditions.

- Others may have just started on their faith journey.

- Never assume that anybody knows anything about the Bible, theology, the church, or your denomination.

- Never assume that parents will be willing or able to explain Bible stories or theological issues to the children.

. . . that kids have a Bible, know Bible stories, or know how to use a Bible.

- At the beginning, make sure everybody has a child-friendly translation of the Bible at home.

- Even "church kids" can be pretty Bible illiterate. Explain any references to Bible characters or stories rather than put a child on the spot about knowing them.

- If your group has several children who don't know how to use a Bible or who don't know the content you expect them to, plan to include some instruction time.

- Consider a special get-together or sleepover to teach Bible skills.

. . . that kids understand or are familiar with worship or prayer.

- Some of your children may not be regular church attenders, especially if you have younger children.

- Some may come from families who are new at this church thing. Coming to church and Sunday school on a weekly basis may be new to them.

- You may need to plan some instruction on behavior during worship services,

on what the elements of worship mean, or on the significance of baptism or Communion.

- You may want to incorporate the Eucharist (the Lord's Supper) into a Sprouts session so you can teach about it.

- Be nonthreatening in inviting the children to pray aloud for the group during Sprouts. Many parents are not comfortable with praying aloud with their families, so this may be a new venture for some children.

- You may want to talk about forms of prayers, times for prayer, or "talking to God" prayers. One model for praying might be to use this acrostic that includes the major types of prayer:

  A is Adoration.
  C is Confession.
  T is Thanksgiving.
  S is Supplication (Making an earnest request)

. . . that kids understand theology or theological terms.

- Kids, like adults, don't want to appear dumb.

- Many won't ask questions.

- Be sure to use kid-friendly language when you discuss issues such as forgiveness, grace, sin, or resurrection.

- Since you will be the mentor, teacher, and model, be sure that you understand and can explain in appropriate ways the theological issues that the group will deal with.

- Keep growing in your own experiences of spiritual formation so that these are not just textbook lessons for the children.

. . . that parents will be supportive.

- Even parents who are church members may not encourage children to do their devotional acts or bring the children to church. You may have to find another adult who can nurture a child or at least provide transportation.

- Parents who are seekers or perhaps non–church members may be even less supportive.

- You may need to write follow-up letters or make phone calls reminding parents of the commitment they made.

- In extreme cases, you will have to wrestle with the difficult issue of what to do with a child who consistently is not keeping the covenant in part or entirely because of unsupportive parents.

. . . that kids will keep confidentiality.

- Deal with this issue at the beginning of Sprouts.

- A note home to parents is also helpful in explaining the confidentiality of the group.

- Explain to parents that if a child wants to talk about what she or he said or did in the group, that is fine. However, parents should not ask the child to tell what others said or did.

. . . Anything!

- Working with children is always surprising, and you should expect the unexpected.

- You may have children who have learning disabilities or who are just uncomfortable reading aloud or writing journal entries. Ask for volunteers unless you already know a child likes to read aloud, and be prepared to assist or understand if a child doesn't want to write during sessions or at home.

- Be as prepared as possible. Make use of the hints and suggestions elsewhere in this book as well as the training materials.

- Be sure to use the tear-out card at the end of this book to become part of the Sprouts network to get continuing ideas and new resources as well as to be in contact with experienced Sprouts leaders. A new issue of *Covenant Discipleship Quarterly* will be sent to your home address four times a year, and information about your church will help us learn about and keep in touch with Sprouts groups across the country.

It's All About Balance

Covenant Discipleship is all about balance. Its focus is on being about the business of both spiritual formation and discipleship living; that is, we must both love God and love our neighbor. It is not one or the other. A plant may produce sprouts, but without the roots of devotion and worship of God, the sprouts will wither. But sprouts that produce no fruits of kindness and justice are also useless and are not fulfilling Jesus' commandments. By practicing the basics of discipleship in all four areas, disciples find balance. They have both healthy roots and life-giving fruit.

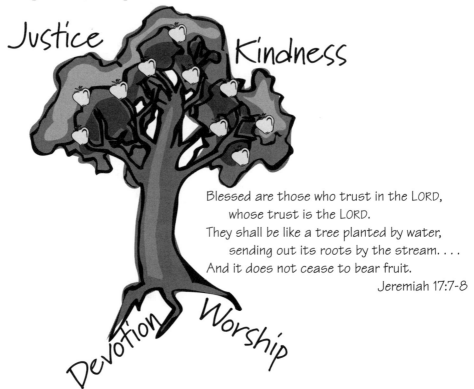

Justice
Kindness

Devotion
Worship

Blessed are those who trust in the LORD,
    whose trust is the LORD.
They shall be like a tree planted by water,
    sending out its roots by the stream. . . .
And it does not cease to bear fruit.
                                        Jeremiah 17:7-8

Many folks seem to put contemplative discipleship and active discipleship in opposition, wanting to choose either "being" or "doing." Covenant Discipleship reminds us that Jesus advocated both and did both. Stories of Jesus, though, also remind us that there are times to act alone and times to be part of a group. Jesus had times of prayer alone, times of community worship, times of healing individuals, and times of addressing unjust systems. There was balance in Jesus' life, and we can strive for balance in the life of a Sprouts group. We simply must remember that balance comes over a period of time, usually not all in one day or during one Sprouts session.

Another balancing act in Covenant Discipleship is that of offering each other forgiveness and grace for unmet commitments, yet still requiring accountability. This balancing act can be difficult. The adult leader plays a key role in helping children learn how and when to be forgiving and when to require and assist members to meet their responsibilities to the covenant. Children will need help in learning what *accountability* means and how it includes a responsibility to encourage and support one another.

Almost all of these statements about balance apply equally to adults, teenagers, or children. However, "a Sprout is not a tree," and there are some differences in dealing with children. While other Covenant Discipleship group meetings consist almost entirely of reporting and discussing the covenant, children need education and assistance in several areas. Depending on your group, children may need instruction in prayer, worship, Bible literacy, or other related areas. All groups will need to learn about justice issues and to carry out justice projects together during Sprouts meetings. Justice is usually a complex and difficult issue even for adults; children need extra help to learn to be justice advocates.

Devotion   **Kindness**

Worship   **Justice**

In the beginning, especially with children unfamiliar with Covenant Discipleship, you will need to spend a good bit of time teaching about the covenant and the basics of discipleship. It will take several weeks to create a covenant and you may spend all or almost all of your time together doing this. Having created their covenant, some groups will be ready to move to a more equal division of Covenant Time and Justice Time. Other groups may need to continue to spend extra time on learning about prayer, worship, or Bible issues with less than half the total time spent on Justice Time. Eventually every group should arrive at a point where Justice Time is receiving significant attention and energy so that all parts of the covenant are being met. Remember, balance comes over a period of time, not all in one day or during one Sprouts session. But balance is the goal.

Life involves being, having, and doing. One of Christianity's tasks is to disclose that what most folks are about is doing for the sake of having a reason for being. But in being gracefully embraced in love by our Lord Jesus Christ . . . what we are about is being for the sake of doing.
W. Paul Jones, *Alive Now,*
January/February 2002, page 49.

For the Sake of Others
Helps for Leading Covenant Time

Christian spiritual formation is the process of being conformed to the image of Christ for the sake of others.[1]

Robert Mulholland

Mulholland emphasizes, as Covenant Discipleship does, that the love of God and the love of others are inextricably intertwined. You just can't have one without the other—at least not if you are going to be a spiritually growing Christian disciple.

Robert Miller uses the analogy of the rhythm of the heart to talk about this relationship.[2] The heart muscle expands, pulling in blood, and then it contracts, pumping blood throughout the body. So we have times of spiritual filling up (loving God: worship and devotion) that prepare us for going out into the world (loving neighbors: kindness and justice). The healthy body needs a heart that expands and contracts; spiritual formation is both an inward journey and an outward journey. We are filled by the Spirit in order to reach out.

The principle described by these examples applies to the process of participation in a covenant group. Each person is spiritually formed by being in a group that provides accountability, and each person is also responsible for providing the same kind of assistance to others. While sharing what they have done and not done, members should always keep in mind not only their own experiences but also how their experiences may benefit the other members of the group in their Christian journeys. Covenant Discipleship groups exist to build up the body of Christ through mutual support and accountability for following all the teachings of Jesus.

Henri Nouwen has written that it is when we are being most personal that we find that we are most universal.[3] We are often surprised that when we, like Paul (Romans 7:14-25), admit our shortcomings and our inability to do what we intend in following God's will, others identify with our plight. In determining what and how to tell others, covenant group members are always asking, "Will others learn from my experience? Is it unique or might others also have this feeling or experience?" The purpose of a Covenant Discipleship group is to be mutually helpful. The struggles, insights, failures, successes, and growth of one group member can impact the spiritual formation of another.

Yes, but "a Sprout is not a tree." The principle of telling our own stories in order to help someone else can be difficult for adults to grasp and carry out. How much more difficult it may be for children. How can adult leaders help children behave in their Covenant Time in such a way that they can require accountability, offer support, and assist others in their spiritual formation?

While you may not teach children this concept directly, you can talk about these values in a general, child-friendly way. As you begin your Sprouts group, you can influence the flow of the Covenant Time in such a way that children learn to respond this way.

Some points to keep in mind:

- *Help children understand that many feelings and experiences are universal.* Each person is not only unique but also similar to others in many ways. In an early Covenant Time, you can help children understand this concept. Let the children list feelings, circumstances, and relationships that people may have. Then let them analyze the lists to determine which ones are common to all people. Which are related only to children? To a youngest child? To children with divorced parents? To children with living grandparents? To children who are afraid of lightning? To children who make friends easily? To children who have been the new kid in school? To children who have wanted to pray about something but didn't know the "right" words?

- *Let children know that the Sprouts Covenant Time group is a safe and confidential group.* In Covenant Time children will tell others about their successes and failures. Trusting that the stories they tell will be kept with confidentiality helps to make the Sprouts group a safe place to express private feelings. And in the process, the children will help one another. Remind them that when we talk with others, we sometimes find out that others are struggling with the same or similar issues. By telling their personal stories, group members may help us, or our stories may help them. You may want to spend some of your Covenant Time discussing some of the issues on the list of feelings, circumstances, and relationships the group has made. Perhaps group members can be helpful to one another in some areas such as divorce, death, making friends, and so forth.

- *Use follow-up inquiries to get the children to give answers that tell more than a simple "yes" or "no."* When children report by saying things like "I read (or did not read) my Bible" or "I picked up (or did not pick up) litter," ask:

  — Why do you think you are having trouble finding time to read your Bible?

  — Why don't you like going to worship?

— What do you like about worship?

— What kinds of prayers are you using?

— Why is it hard to be kind to your brother?

— Why do you think people are afraid of homeless folks?

— What are you learning from your Bible reading?

— How can we help you fulfill this covenant clause that you're having trouble with?

- *When appropriate, tell the children about your own struggles or victories.* While adults must use discretion in telling children about adult issues, it is also possible and helpful to let children know that adults are not perfect. They haven't arrived at some magical point in spiritual formation and stopped growing. Let the children know that you too have failures and slip-ups, as well as successes.

Endnotes

1 From *Shaped by the Word,* Rev. ed. © 1985, 2000 by Robert Mulholland, Jr. Used by permission of Upper Room Books. From page 25.

2 See *Fire in the Deep,* by Robert J. Miller, Lectio Divina Series, Cycle A (Sheed & Ward, 2001), pages 65-66.

3 See *Bread for the Journey: A Daybook of Wisdom and Faith,* by Henri J. M. Nouwen (HarperSanFrancisco, 1997), entry for February 23.

Justice: Understanding, Implementing It

The Trouble With Justice

Several years ago I (Steve Manskar) helped form a Covenant Discipleship group at Lanesboro United Methodist Church. We began with the General Rule of Discipleship: *"To witness to Jesus Christ in the world, and to follow his teachings through acts of compassion, justice, worship, and devotion, under the guidance of the Holy Spirit."*[1] Our covenant's preamble and the clauses covering compassion, worship, and devotion were completed without much difficulty. But a problem arose when we began discussing Acts of Justice; most of the group didn't understand what Acts of Justice were. More importantly, they weren't sure what the term *justice* meant within the context of the General Rule of Discipleship. We resolved our difficulty by adding the following clause to our covenant: "I will engage in study with this group to gain a biblical understanding of justice."

Justice Comes in Last

I have been involved with many Covenant Discipleship groups over the years. Each put much prayer and effort into writing their covenants. Once the covenant was written and signed, each group shared at least one common characteristic: all encountered difficulty coming to grips with Acts of Justice.

The difficulty with justice clauses was made visible by their location within the covenants themselves; they were always placed last. Placing these clauses last not only indicated the groups' uneasiness with understanding their meaning and application, it also meant that those clauses would not be covered if the meeting ran over the allotted hour.

This leads me to believe that Acts of Justice is the least understood and least implemented portion of many covenants. I believe this is true for at least two reasons. First, justice is often confused with compassion. Acts of Compassion (Kindness) involve personal works of love toward the neighbor who is in need.

Acts of Justice address the systems that cause the neighbor's need. Justice is compassion expanded to the whole community. Acts of Compassion are personal and private, while Acts of Justice are social and public.

Secondly, Acts of Justice require us to write, say, and do things that are often unpopular and risky. Being an agent for justice involves asking questions and taking actions that may make people you care about uncomfortable or angry. Acts of Justice take us into the community to challenge the status quo. Just as Jesus challenged the status quo of first-century Jerusalem and found himself on a Roman cross, those who proclaim and act on his good news of justice for the least, the last, and the lost today risk being "crucified" as well.

The Crux of Human Relationships

How are we to understand justice within the context of the General Rule of Discipleship? The Hebrew word *mispat* (pronounced "mishpāt") is commonly translated as "justice" or "judgment." *Mispat* is an attribute of God that governs God's relationship with humankind. As humankind is created in God's image, *mispat* provides the foundation upon which human communities are formed. Bruce Birch gives this helpful definition: "The *mišpat* of God is experienced by the vulnerable in the community as 'justice,' the upholding of their rights, and the advocacy of their need (Deut. 10:18; Ps. 10:18; Jer. 5:28). To those who have denied or manipulated the rights of others God's *mišpat* may be translated as 'judgment,' the activity of God to hold accountable those who exploit the rights of others."[2]

Justice forms the crux of humankind's relationship with God and with one another. It creates and sustains community by assuring that everyone is provided an opportunity to be a full participant in community life. Acts of Justice become necessary when people are excluded. They address the causes of the oppression and exclusion of the weakest and most vulnerable members of the community. The purpose of Acts of Justice is to restore *shalom* (wholeness and peace) to individual and community life.

Justice is at the center of the gospel of Christ. In the Beatitudes (Matthew 5:1-12; Luke 6:20-23) we find Jesus describing life in the community of God's kingdom. In both versions of the Beatitudes, Jesus informs his disciples of God's special concern for those who are rejected and cast aside by the world: the poor, the hungry, those who mourn, the meek, those who thirst for righteousness, the merciful, the peacemakers, and the persecuted. In accord with God's *mispat*, these weak and vulnerable ones are assured a place in God's community. And God requires that they be given their rightful place in the human community.

In Luke 4:16-21, Jesus reads from Isaiah 61:1-2 and delivers his mission statement to the world. He announces:

The Spirit of the Lord is upon me,
because he has anointed me
   to bring good news to the poor.
He has sent me to proclaim release to the captives
   and recovery of sight to the blind,
   to let the oppressed go free,
to proclaim the year of the Lord's favor.

Luke 4:18-19

The Shalom That Justice Brings

Jesus came to fulfill Isaiah's words. Everything he did and said on his way to the cross was in service of his mission of revealing the divine community known as the Kingdom of God. Jesus did this by creating communities everywhere he went, communities in which the poor, the outcasts, the sick, the disabled, widows, sinners, and tax collectors were assured a place at the table. The community he left behind is known to us as the church. Therefore, the church is called to be a community that lives out God's *mispat* in its life in the world.

Acts of Justice take us into the life of our community. They call us to become aware of the issues arising from life in our towns, cities, states, the nation, and the world. When we see the needs of the poorest and most vulnerable citizens ignored, God's *mispat* calls us to speak out and to act. Acts of Justice are means of grace that build and restore community. The good news of Christ is revealed in the wholeness *(shalom)* that justice brings.

Perhaps now we can understand why justice is such a difficult and neglected, albeit essential, part of our covenants and why Acts of Justice follow Acts of Compassion (Kindness) in the General Rule of Discipleship. As faithful disciples of Jesus Christ, we must challenge ourselves and our Covenant Discipleship groups to place the justice clauses nearer to the top of our covenants. Justice is essential for our lives as disciples of Jesus Christ and members of the family of God.

Endnotes

1 From *Guide for Covenant Discipleship Groups,* by Gayle Turner Watson (Discipleship Resources, 2000), page 12. See also *The Book of Discipline— 2000,* ¶ 1116.2a.

2 From Bruce C. Birch, *Let Justice Roll Down: The Old Testament, Ethics, and Christian Life* (Louisville: Westminster/John Knox Press, 1991), page 156.

An earlier version of this article appeared in *Covenant Discipleship Quarterly,* volume 11, number 3 (Spring 1995).

Kid-Friendly Language

And yet again: "A Sprout is not a tree."

Since Sprouts is derived from the forms of adult Covenant Discipleship groups, you will need to do some transposing into kid-friendly language upon occasion. Remember that some terminology of the adult Covenant Discipleship has already been changed in this book to make the language more accessible for children (see page 8). Here are some age-level language issues you will want to keep in mind.

Fairness / Justice

In the beginning, use the word *fairness* to help children understand the word *justice*. Most children understand and use the phrase "It isn't fair!" Help them to see that injustice occurs when things are not fair. When you have this conversation, you should probably plan for some time for the children to tell you about things that aren't fair in their lives.

Justice, however, is more than merely fairness. Once the children have made the connection between fairness and justice, they can begin to understand the deeper levels of justice. For example, they can begin to consider that justice may require going beyond simple fairness in order to correct a wrong.

Piety, Mercy, Compassion / Loving God and Neighbor, Kindness

While the more kid-friendly words (*loving God, loving neighbor, kindness*) are essential to helping children understand the concepts, it is also important for the children—especially the older ones—to hear the adult words and begin to make some connections with their meanings. The more child-friendly terms lose a little of the richness and depth of the adult words, so you will want to help the children, as they are ready, to get a feel for the full meanings of *piety, mercy,* and *compassion.*

Theological Concepts

Invariably, theological issues will arise in Sprouts groups. Children will ask questions such as "Why doesn't prayer work?" (that is,

why did someone I prayed for not get well or even die?). Additionally, as children learn more about Bible study and about worship, issues will come up relating to these, too.

It will not always be easy to translate these complex and mysterious topics into terms and explanations understandable to a third or even a sixth grader. There may be some concepts that you are still struggling with as an adult. But it will be up to you to provide some kind of response. However, do not be afraid to admit that you do not know an answer or that you struggle with the same question. Children need to know that theological questions will always be part of the Christian experience.

Many of the Sprouts will still be concrete thinkers. No matter how well you explain, they may not be able to conceptualize some abstractions such as grace, the Trinity, forgiveness, or unanswered prayer. Be sure that you use specific examples and stories when you can. Repeat some of Jesus' parables when they are appropriate. Do your best.

Remember that sometimes the best or only answer is, "This is the best I can do. Some things we just don't understand/can't explain. Some things are part of the mystery of God."

Although you might feel the urge to simplify these matters, never give information that is wrong or a theory that will have to be unexplained at a later date (such as using the term *sleep* in explaining death or saying that God took a child to be an angel or responding that prayers weren't answered because of lack of faith).

Children / Kids / Young People

As children get older—especially as they near adolescence—they no longer want to be referred to as *children.* You can respect their feelings without allowing them the status of adults. Consider using the terms *kids, young people,* or *boys and girls* rather than *children.*

Your Language Reflects Your Situation

Sprouts is designed for children in grades three through six. Some churches have included mature second graders and some have used it with seventh graders as a bridge to youth groups. Some churches have included several grade levels and others have only one grade in a Sprouts group. You will have to adapt the suggestions in this book for your group. There can be a great deal of difference not only between third graders and sixth graders but also among children of the same age. Be sure your language, expectations, and activities are appropriate for your children. And remember, the concepts of accountability and covenant may be beyond the understanding of children younger than third grade.

Remember the Older Children

Sprouts encourages older elementary-age children to use some skills, undertake some responsibilities, and encounter some concepts that many of them have not yet experienced. Remember that just as you strive to use language that is fully accessible to children, you will also want to help children grow and develop by having new experiences. Once they have grasped the child-friendly words, introduce them to the adult words. Do not expect them to use the adult words easily, but encourage them to recognize the adult words when they hear them.

Baptized and Professing Members

What does Sprouts have to do with baptism and profession of faith?
"Baptism and profession of faith is what Sprouts is all about!"

The meaning and power of baptism are described in the introduction to the Baptismal Covenant:

> Through the Sacrament of Baptism
>   we are initiated into Christ's holy church.
> We are incorporated into God's mighty acts of salvation
>   and given new birth through water and the Spirit.
> All this is God's gift, offered to us without price.[1]

The sacrament of baptism is God's action for and with us within the family of believers called the church. It is the gift of God's unconditional love and acceptance. Baptism is the door to life in God's household, including life in the Spirit and the sharing of the family meal.[2] It is the way God initiates us into the family of God's Son, Jesus Christ. Through baptism we are initiated into the reign of God in the world and "made to share in Christ's royal priesthood."[3]

Because baptism is God's act, all who receive this gift of water and the Spirit are fully members of God's household, the church. Every person who is baptized is received as a member of the church of Jesus Christ. In The United Methodist Church all baptized infants and children are placed on the roll as baptized members.

As we continue reading in the Baptismal Covenant, we see that this gift from God is also a way of life. Through the waters of baptism, God promises to always accept, love, and forgive us. With the power of the Holy Spirit, God marks each of us as God's own daughter or son. In response, whether we can answer for ourselves at baptism or as we mature following baptism in infancy, we promise to give our lives and loyalty to God and to God's family in the church. In other words, when we receive the water of baptism, God marks us as God's own, gives us a new name (Christian), a new family (the church), and a new way of life (Jesus Christ), joined to his death and resurrection.[4]

After proper instruction and formation in the Christian faith and life, baptized members may affirm the baptismal and membership vows for themselves through a profession of faith.[5] This profession is their first and continuing profession of the faith and a promise to live for the reign of God's mercy and justice. At that time they become not only baptized members of the church but also professing members.

Sprouts and Church Membership

When a child is baptized, parents and sponsors promise to nurture the child in Christian faith by their teaching and example. The local congregation promises to surround the child with a community of love and forgiveness, to pray for the child, and to nurture and instruct the child so that he or she may grow in faith and love. Sprouts is a way parents and the congregation can keep the promises they make at the baptism of their children.

Sprouts is a proven and effective way of instructing children in Christian faith and life by teaching children the basics of discipleship: kindness, justice, worship, and devotion. In the support and accountability of Covenant Time and Justice Time each week, children develop holy habits that nurture their faith and form them as disciples of Jesus Christ who are ready to affirm the baptismal vows for themselves and become professing members of The United Methodist Church and witnesses to the reign of God.

Through Sprouts, children can discover what it means to make a lifelong commitment to God as a professing member of the church. Sprouts leaders can build into each session some opportunity for children to live out the vows they will take when they become professing members.[6] These activities may be as simple as putting someone's name on a prayer list; signing that they are present and listing another time that week they have been to church; contributing money, food, clothes, or other goods for others; reading the Bible regularly; or listing a way they have served someone else during each week. These actions may well be a part of the group covenant created by the Sprouts. However, when the Sprouts leader ties the actions to the practice of the vows of professing membership, Sprouts can make the connection between their Sprouts activities and a lifelong commitment as a professing member of God's church.

To learn more about the meaning of baptism, see:

Baptism: Christ's Act in the Church, by Laurence Hull Stookey (Abingdon Press, 1982).

By Water and the Spirit: Making Connections for Identity & Ministry, by Gayle Carlton Felton (Discipleship Resources, 2002).

Living Hope: Baptism and the Cost of Christian Witness, by Robin Maas (Discipleship Resources, 1999).

Remember Who You Are: Baptism, a Model for Christian Life, by William H. Willimon (Upper Room, 1980).

Endnotes

1 From Baptismal Covenants I, II © 1976, 1980, 1985, 1989 The United Methodist Publishing House. In *The United Methodist Hymnal* (United Methodist Publishing House, 1989), pages 33 and 39.

2 See "The Baptismal Covenant," in *The United Methodist Hymnal* (United Methodist Publishing House, 1989), pages 37 and 39.

3 From Baptismal Covenants I, II © 1976, 1980, 1985, 1989 The United Methodist Publishing House. In *The United Methodist Hymnal* (United Methodist Publishing House, 1989), pages 37 and 43. See also 1 Peter 2:9.

4 See "The Baptismal Covenant," in *The United Methodist Hymnal* (United Methodist Publishing House, 1989), pages 34, 36, and 37.

5 See "The Baptismal Covenant," in *The United Methodist Hymnal* (United Methodist Publishing House, 1989), pages 34 and 38.

6 See *The United Methodist Book of Discipline, 2000,* ¶ 216.

Children and Justice: Age-Level Characteristics

Characteristics of Grades 3-6	Implications for Teaching
Concrete thinking; fifth and sixth graders developing abstract thinking skills	Provide hands-on learning experiences. Use familiar language in addition to building children's religious vocabulary. Use open-ended stories to help children consider choices for action and connect their actions with what they believe/think.
Ability to categorize information into time and space	Have children research customs, languages, religion, or other information related to another country. Provide books or videos about a variety of people and cultures. Sponsor field trips to learn about other people and issues that affect them.
Growing ability to recognize cause and effect	Use stories and experiences from daily life to talk about the correlation between actions and the effects those actions have on other people.
Importance of friends, especially same-sex groups	Let friends work together, but encourage respect for all persons. Use conversation about friendship to broaden their understanding of *neighbor, compassion,* and *justice.*
Enjoyment of being part of a group, club, or other organized activity	Plan group fundraisers. Organize group service projects. Talk about the necessity of all people working together to bring about justice and to change systems.
Independence; growing ability to recognize interdependence of human beings and the natural world	Provide opportunities for children to make choices; ask questions to help them form and articulate their opinions. Work as teams to create solutions to problems.
Increased ability to understand other people's perspectives	Use role-play, group discussion, and other experiences to help children understand and appreciate other viewpoints.
Growing sense of justice and equality	Encourage cooperative learning. Provide opportunities for hands-on service to others. Explore justice issues facing your community or state.
Increased awareness of the global nature of society	Provide opportunities to be in service to others within the congregation, community, and world.

What's the Difference Between Kindness and Justice?

A justice issue is an issue that develops because a part of God's creation (people, animals, or the earth) is not being treated fairly—with love and care. A justice issues arises when equal value is not placed on all persons or there is not harmony among people or creation. Examples of justice issues are hunger, homelessness, people being treating unfairly because they are of a different race or religion, or unwise use of natural resources. As Christians, we can respond to issues that concern us through both Acts of Kindness and Acts of Justice. What, though, is the difference between kindness and justice?

An Act of Kindness is a helpful response to immediate need.
An Act of Justice goes beyond helping the immediate need to making a change in a situation or system in order to correct the causes of the problem so that all creation is treated with fairness and respect.

KINDNESS IS:

helping someone you know

helping someone you don't know

helping before you are asked

making someone feel better

giving up something you want to make someone else happy

giving up something of yours for someone else

sharing

JUSTICE IS:

changing your behavior toward others

encouraging someone else to change behavior in order to help a situation

making a friend out of an enemy

working to make a bad situation better

finding ways to change an unjust system

making the world a better place

educating yourself and others about a justice issue

ACTS OF KINDNESS:

("Giving a hungry person a fish")

Giving used clothing to a person who is homeless

Giving money to Heifer Project International

Being nice to a schoolmate who is "different"

Taking a "Say No to Drugs" pledge

Collecting plastic rings from soda cans to recycle

Picking up litter

ACTS OF JUSTICE:

("Teaching a hungry person to fish")

Opening a Clothes Closet at your church for people who are homeless

Making a poster, bulletin insert, or announcement in church telling about Heifer Project International, encouraging others to help raise funds

Defending a schoolmate who is "different"

Convincing your friends to take a "Say No to Drugs" pledge

Implementing a plastic-ring recycling project

Writing letters to Congress asking for a bottle-return law

Part 4

Sprouts

Let the little children come to me, and do not
stop them; for it is to such as these that
the kingdom of heaven belongs.
Matthew 19:14

Plan Your First Sprouts Meeting

1. Begin With Group-Building
- Your first Sprouts meeting may be in one group. Plan to break up into smaller Covenant Time groups at your second meeting.
- Be sure that everyone knows the names of all the children and adults in the group.
- To make a game of it, after each introduction, let the person name another person (real or fictional) that they would want to be like. Have them explain why. (Be sure that the leader participates as a part of the group.)

2. Talk About What It Means to Be a Disciple
- Ask: "What does the word *disciple* mean?" (follower, part of a group, a learner, and so forth)
- Ask: "What does it mean to be a disciple of Jesus Christ?" (follow God's commandments, love God and neighbor, go to church and/or Sunday school, be a Christian, read the Bible, pray, and so forth)

3. Explain the Purpose of the Sprouts Group
- Explain that the Sprouts group will be a place where the boys and girls, along with their adult leaders, can help one another become more faithful disciples of Jesus Christ.
- Hand out copies of the examples of works of Loving Neighbors and Loving God (page 35). Talk about the four kinds of Acts that are a part of the Sprouts experience. Read some of the examples from the sheet.
- Explain that each Sprouts session will be divided into two parts: Covenant Time and Justice Time.
- In Covenant Time, small groups will talk about how they have been disciples during the week. They will talk about how they are growing in their relationship to God, and they will pray together. They will talk about their Acts of Worship and their Acts of Devotion.
- In Justice Time, Sprouts will learn about justice issues that are important in their own lives and in the world. They will have opportunities to plan and carry out Acts of Kindness and Acts of Justice.

4. Learn About the Group Covenant
- Tell the group that the discussions in their smaller Covenant Time groups will be guided by a covenant that each group will make together over the next few weeks.
- Help the children to understand that a covenant is an agreement about what each child will do during the week between covenant meetings as long as the Sprouts meetings continue. The Sprouts covenant will include agreements about how the members of the group will practice works of Loving Neighbors and Loving God.
- Encourage the children to brainstorm possible Acts of Worship and

Acts of Devotion. (Explain that they will talk about the Acts of Kindness and Acts of Justice during Justice Time, later in the meeting.)

- Remind them that they are not writing a covenant today, but they are brainstorming all kinds of ideas about what they may want to include in their smaller group's covenant later.

- Tell the children that when they write their group covenant, they will agree on one or two Acts for each category for the whole group to perform.

- Assure them that each person will also be able to add one or two personal acts to her or his covenant.

- Ask the children to continue to think during the coming week about possibilities of Acts they would like to include in their group covenant.

5. Create a Sprouts Journal
(Save the journal for the next week's meeting if time is short.)

- Use the ideas on pages 56–57 to select a method for creating the Sprouts journals.

- Explain that although the group does not yet have a completed covenant, the children can use the pages of their journals to write down the Acts they do during the next week. They can also record their prayer requests and write down any Bible verses they read during the week, along with any thoughts about the Bible verses.

6. Review What It Means to Be a Covenant Group

- Remind the children that their Sprouts group is a covenant group. They will work together and support one another as they grow to become better disciples of Jesus Christ.

- Remind them that the Sprouts group will be a place where they can say what they feel and ask questions without having anyone laugh at them or make fun of them.

- Remind them that everything they say during the Covenant Time of a Sprouts meeting is confidential, which means it will not be repeated to anyone else. Tell the group that keeping things confidential is one of the covenant agreements they make.

- Remind them that their purpose will be to help one another become more faithful disciples of Jesus Christ.

7. End Covenant Time With Prayer

- If the children have made their journals, encourage them to write their prayer requests there.

- Close Covenant Time with a prayer for the children as they grow in their relationship to God and to one another.

8. Serve a Snack

- Let the children have a break between Covenant Time and Justice Time.

- Remember that even the snacks you choose will teach the children something about being faithful disciples. Choose snacks that are simple, inexpensive, and nutritious. Fruit, pretzels, and real fruit juices are good. Avoid the less nutritious water and juice products.

- Avoid environmentally wasteful packaging such as individually packaged drinks or snacks.

- Whenever possible, plan snacks that are relevant to the lesson plan. (Since this is the first session, there may be no specific snack that relates, but in other sessions there may be.)

9. Follow Up With Justice Time

- Remember that you may have several smaller Covenant Groups meeting together for Justice Time.

- Explain that in Justice Time, the group will discover ways that they can practice being disciples by showing kindness and justice to others.

- Hand out copies of "What's the Difference Between Kindness and Justice?" (page 49). Use the examples on the sheet to talk about the difference between Acts of Kindness and Acts of Justice.

- Acknowledge that the distinction between kindness and justice is not always easy to make. Assure the children that they will learn more about Acts of Kindness and Acts of Justice as they work together.

- Encourage the children to brainstorm possible Acts of Kindness and Acts of Justice.

- Remind them that they are not writing a covenant today, but they are brainstorming all kinds of ideas about what they may want to include in Justice Time each week.

- Remind the children that when they write their group covenant, they will agree on one or two Acts for each category for the whole group to perform.

- Each Sprout will, of course, also be able to add some personal Acts if he or she wishes.

- Ask the children to continue to think during the coming week about possibilities for Acts they would like to include in their group covenant.

10. Close With Prayer

- Invite the children to participate by naming their special concerns or by writing them on a sheet of paper and dropping it in a box on the worship table. (Be sure to destroy the written prayer requests, without reading them, as soon as the session is over.)

- Close with a simple prayer for God's presence with the children and leaders of the Sprouts group as they learn and grow together. Include a prayer for the individual prayer requests made by the members of the group.

- Encourage the children to look forward to fun ways to learn and grow together.

Plan the Weekly Covenant Time

Each week's session will be roughly broken into two sections: Covenant Time and Justice Time. You can use the Session-Planning Sheet (page 65) to help you plan.

At the second meeting of the Sprouts, form your Covenant Time groups of no more than six Sprouts per group. Each group can use the brainstorming ideas from the first session to get them started as they develop their own Covenant Time group covenant.

Covenant Time lasts for approximately forty-five minutes. For the first few weeks a significant portion of Covenant Time will be spent developing the group's own covenant.

Developing the Group Covenant

- **Covenant Basics:** Begin with the General Rule of Discipleship, which is the starting point for all Covenant Discipleship covenants—"To witness to Jesus Christ in the world, and to follow his teachings through acts of compassion [kindness], justice, worship, and devotion, under the guidance of the Holy Spirit."[1]

- Start where the children are in their faith development; do not base the group covenant on where you believe the children *ought* to be.

- Remind the children that the covenant is a statement of some of their intentions for living as disciples of Jesus Christ, but their actions as Christian disciples may involve more than they include in this one covenant.

- Tell the children that the covenant is a living document, which means that it can change and grow as the Sprouts grow in their understanding of the Covenant Discipleship process.

- **The Parts of the Covenant:** The covenant will have three essential parts—(1) a preamble, (2) the clauses, and (3) a conclusion.

- In addition, each Sprout may add personal clauses for growing as a Christian disciple in her or his own life.

- **The Preamble:** The preamble will make it clear that the children are not establishing a set of rules. Instead, the covenant is a statement of shared faith in Jesus Christ and a naming of ways in which Sprouts can express their love for God and love for neighbor. The preamble makes it clear that the group's ability to live as Christian disciples, fulfilling the clauses of their covenant, is possible because of the grace of God.

- For the first meeting you may have a sample preamble for the group's covenant (see page 66). When the covenant is complete, though, the children may want to write their own preamble.

- **The Covenant Clauses:** The clauses of the covenant (no more than eight to ten) should be balanced between Acts of Kindness, Justice, Worship, and Devotion. Each clause must be as simple and specific as possible and limited to acts that everyone is willing and able to do.

- The members of the group should become familiar with Acts of Kindness, Justice, Worship, and Devotion. Use the "Loving Neighbors/Loving

God" sheet (page 35) and "What's the Difference Between Kindness and Justice?" (page 49) often as the children make decisions about which Acts will become part of their group covenant.

- Encourage personal clauses for Sprouts who have special needs or interests. However, not everyone will want to add a personal clause.
- **The Covenant Conclusion:** End the covenant with a statement that reaffirms the nature and purpose of the covenant and emphasizes again the supreme importance of grace in Christian discipleship.
- **The Completed Covenant:** Use the blank covenant form on page 67 to create the final group covenant. Have each child and adult leader sign a copy of the covenant for each member of the group.
- Then each group member can sign the personal covenant section at the bottom of his or her own copy of the covenant.
- Encourage those who want to add a personal clause to write that clause under the appropriate Acts section. (Keep a list of the personal clauses so that you can encourage the child to be faithful to that clause as well as to the entire group covenant.)
- Once the group has created its covenant, each child should have a copy to keep in his or her journal.

Creating and Using the Sprouts Journal

- Choose a method for creating the Sprouts journal. Leaders who have taught children before will probably have their own favorite way of creating a journal. Some possibilities include report folders or small three-ring notebooks. If hole-punching is not convenient, you can staple the journal pages together between two sheets of construction paper. Another option might be to let the Sprouts collect the loose pages of their journal in a folder each week and then make their own individual cover at the end of the Sprouts term.
- You may have all the pages of the journal available when the journal is begun. Or you may plan to provide a new sheet to be added to the journal at each session.
- Whatever method you choose to create the journal, include two pages, printed back and front on one sheet of paper, for each week.

  Side 1: A dated page for recording works of Loving Neighbors and Loving God that were accomplished that week and prayer requests for themselves and others in their group (sample, page 70);

  Side 2: A Bible study page (sample, page 71) for recording Bible verses they read, along with what they have learned or the questions they have. If you know what Bible verses you will want the children to read each week, write the reference(s) on the picture at the top of the page. If you leave the book space blank, you can have the children write in the Bible references for the next week at the end of Covenant Time each week.

- There will not be time for the children to make their own journals, but you may want to allow a little time for them to decorate their individual covers. Their own added touch will create a more personal ownership for the journal and for the things they will be writing in the journals.

- Add the cover to the journal when it is made, or plan a time for covers to be added at the last meeting of the Covenant Time group, when the journals are complete. Be sure the cover has a place for the name of the Sprout who owns the journal (sample, page 69).

- Encourage the children to write in their journals each week. They will be using the journals to guide their conversation during Covenant Time.

- Encourage all of the children to write in the journals each week, but do not worry about the child who does not write as long as the child is participating in the group.

Leading Covenant Time

- At the beginning of each Covenant Time, read aloud your covenant as a group.

- During the session, ask each child to describe the Acts she or he has performed in each of the areas (kindness, justice, worship, devotion) during the last week. Be sure to tell about your own Acts.

- Remember that some children may not have Acts to report in every area every week. However, encourage the Sprouts to include Acts in all four areas regularly.

- If any of the children have added a personal clause to the covenant, make sure you have written it down. If a Sprout does not mention his or her clause, ask about it.

- In the beginning, you may need to help children be supportive of one another. Some children will take failures extremely seriously. They will need to be reassured that God forgives them and that they just need to keep trying.

- Others may not take the covenant seriously enough. Ask questions that will help them think about and articulate what they might do to be faithful to the covenant.

- Depending on time available for Covenant Time, you may also choose to discuss the Bible verses the children have read—especially if they have written notes on the Bible study page in their journals.

- There are several ways to select verses that will encourage the children to read Scripture in an organized way:
  - Reading the Gospel lesson from the weekly lectionary readings
  - Handing out a bookmark with a Bible verse on it
  - Selecting verses related to the justice issue for the week

- When you read Scripture aloud during Covenant Time, be sensitive to children who don't feel comfortable reading aloud. The goal is to help children develop Bible reading as a personal Act of Devotion. Keep in touch with parents, and be happy to hear from parents that their children are reading the Bible more often than they did before joining Sprouts.

Closing Covenant Time

- Ask the children about how their prayers have been answered during the previous week. Concentrate specifically on prayer concerns that were discussed during Covenant Time the week before.

- Ask for today's prayer concerns.

- Encourage the children to write the requests in their journals so that they can pray for their group's concerns during the week.

- Close with prayer. At first you may need to say the prayer, but after the group has been meeting for a while, invite the children to offer sentence prayers.

Plan the Weekly Justice Time

Planning and implementing the justice sessions is the most time-consuming part of a Sprouts program. Justice involves change. Almost by definition, changing a system, situation, or person requires more time, effort, and determination than simply meeting an immediate need (an Act of Kindness). Children will seldom be able to address the whole system of a problem, but they can respond to a part of it or effect a change in others' understanding or behavior.

Children need to be taught that God requires us to care for those who are hungry, who need clothes, who are in prison, or who do not have a home (Deuteronomy 10:17-19; 24:17-22; Isaiah 58:6-14; Matthew 25:31-46). Then children need assistance in determining what they can do to show their care. The most effective way to approach this is to spend time educating the children about a justice issue and then presenting some ways for them to respond.

Unless children are encouraged and supported, however, they will not be able to carry out Acts of Justice in any sustained way. In the beginning it will probably be best for you to choose the justice issue for the group, letting them know the reason for your selection. After several terms of Sprouts meetings, though, experienced Sprouts may be able to express an interest in a justice issue on their own. (See pages 61–63 for more discussion about choosing a justice issue for Justice Time.)

Remember that children may have difficulty empathizing with problems if they have not experienced them. Some children may express prejudice against people who are different from them. Other children may have experienced painful situations of being discriminated against or being in need. In all cases you will need be sensitive about how you handle Justice Time. Remember we must always join with those who are experiencing pain in solving the difficulties rather than patronizing those whom we want to help.

Justice Time provides an excellent opportunity for Sprouts children to

- develop a sense of belonging, while learning to be inclusive of those who are different;

- learn mutual respect;
- practice forgiveness;
- struggle with difficult moral issues and confront their own prejudices;
- respond to a concern with action that makes a difference;
- stand up for others and dare to be different from their peers;
- develop the skills, sensitivity, and caring necessary for becoming advocates for those in need.

Don't be surprised if you have to point out the differences between kindness and justice on a regular basis. Generally, you may describe kindness as an action that helps another person. Justice, on the other hand, is an action that brings about a change to make things better or more fair. Fairness is a concept that children understand well. Although justice is a bigger issue than simple fairness, making the connection between justice and fairness is a good place to start. Ultimately, though, it is less important to emphasize understanding the difference between justice and kindness than it is to encourage children to include both kinds of Acts in their covenant.

Keep the "What's the Difference Between Kindness and Justice?" sheet close at hand during Justice Time. You and the children may need to refer to it often!

Here are ten suggestions for helping you to plan your Justice Time:

1. Review "What's the Difference Between Kindness and Justice?" on page 49.

2. Identify resource people who can help you with information about specific justice issues: chairpersons of Church and Society, Health and Welfare, or Missions ministry areas; United Methodist Women or United Methodist Men program chairpersons; directors of community agencies (agencies dealing with hunger or other issues); a community organizer; pastors; directors of Christian education or children's ministries.

3. Contact your annual conference media center to locate available video or film resources.

4. Use ideas from resources listed in "Resources for Additional Planning," beginning on page 91.

5. Contact Curric-U-Phone (800-251-8591) and ask for suggestions for resources to use with a specific issue.

6. Include active projects, such as serving in a soup kitchen.

7. Participate in mission and service projects already planned for your congregation.

8. Have children prepare a presentation on a justice issue to educate the congregation (posters, skits, a bulletin board, and so forth).

9. Limit costs related to participating in a particular activity, emphasizing that good stewardship is a justice issue too.

10. Let the children help decide what issues they want to explore through study and action.

As you plan for Justice Time, remember that children are concrete thinkers. Use illustrations and graphs to help them identify on a feeling level with statistics related to a justice issue. For example, here are two ways to illustrate a point about a justice issue.

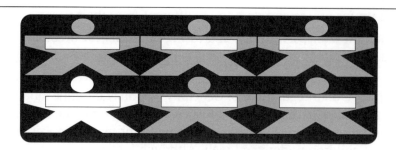

Instructions
Write the name of a child you know on each figure. You may use your own name if you want.

Did You Know?
In the United States, one out of every six children is poor and hungry. That means that the child whose name is on the above white figure represents someone who is poor and hungry.

Figure 1

Figure 2 below uses a bar graph to help children visualize how U.S. citizens spend their money.

How U.S. Citizens Spent Their Money
Americans spent $34 billion on fast food at McDonald's, Burger King, and Wendy's in 2001.

The government spent $4 billion on the Special Supplemental Food Program for Women, Infants, and Children (WIC) in 2001.

McDonald's, Burger King, Wendy's   WIC
(Each square represents $1,000,000,000 spent.)

Figure 2

You will find additional ideas for activities and session plans in Part 5 of this book, beginning on page 77. Adapt those ideas to meet your needs or use them as a guide for developing your own plans for Justice Time.

Choosing Themes for Justice Time

There are many things to consider when choosing the justice issue that your Sprouts group will be working with. You may want to choose the first justice issue for the group. Here are some possibilities for justice issues to begin with.

- **World Peace**—Look for ways to promote peace. First, the group will need to discuss and define what peace is. Include not only global peace but also peace in the homes, schools, cities, and churches of the Sprouts. As the Sprouts are able to understand the discussion, expand the ideas to what it means to have peace within yourself. Next, decide how to make peace a justice issue. Will you teach someone about peace? Will you do a survey to find out what others think about peace? Will you read the book *Sadako and the Thousand Paper Cranes* and then fold origami cranes to distribute throughout your city for display with information about peace?

- **World Hunger**—Introduce the issue of world hunger as an opportunity for understanding how God calls us to care for others. The group may choose to include both projects to provide food for hungry people and projects to raise their own and others' awareness of the needs of people who do not have enough to eat. For example, the group can use a concordance to search for all of the verses in the Bible that tell us to care for others or about people who are hungry. Perhaps it would be helpful for the Sprouts to experience hunger for themselves. Hold a lock-in. Let your group invite friends. One group came together and began their event eating a meal together. Then they attended the Maundy Thursday Service at church. Their last meal together before they fasted was the Lord's Supper. Then the fast began. They only drank water and juice and ate some popsicles and jello. They recorded how they felt every few hours. They kept busy with various activities:

  — a scavenger hunt throughout their church building gathering facts about hunger;

  — a visit from a worker at a local food bank;

  — a scavenger hunt for food from people in the neighborhood surrounding the church that would be donated to the food bank;

  — and yes, they even took some time to have fellowship, watch some movies, and have some fun.

At the end of the event the group discussed how their behaviors had changed as they became more and more hungry. This allowed them not only to feel hunger but to experience the change in emotions that occurred as the hunger overtook them. They ended the event after twenty-four hours by eating a meal together and then attending the Good Friday Service. It was an eye-opening experience for the Sprouts and for their leaders.

- **Internet Safety**—Many people, both adults and kids, are not aware of the dangers on the Internet. But they should be. Even the daily news reports prove to us that unless Internet users follow some guidelines, the Internet is not a safe place to be. Chat rooms are often not occupied by the best of characters. One Sprouts group did some research on the topic of Internet safety. They invited their local law enforcement officials to come to give them information. Then they developed their own Internet safety brochure to distribute in their local schools to educate others about the dangers of the Internet and to help them learn how to be safe on the Internet.

- **Bullying**—One group dealt with the topic of bullying in their local schools. What should you do if an adult is the one picking on you? What do you do if your group of friends are the ones doing the bullying? Who should you tell? Should you just keep quiet? These questions—plus many more—were issues the Sprouts could deal with. So they did some research; they read some books; they checked the Bible for answers; and they even watched a movie on the topic. Then they wrote scripts and made videos that would help to answer their questions. They showed these videos to others to provide a valuable tool for discussions among students. (You may be able to involve a local high school student as a consultant for the video-making process.)

- **Other Possible Topics:**
    - **Homelessness** (Try living in a parking lot in a box overnight);
    - **Conflict Resolution** (How do you address conflicts in a positive way?);
    - **Prejudice** (Improve relations between religious, racial, or ethnic groups);
    - **Student Mentors** (Help to provide a mentoring program involving older students with younger students who are having problems);
    - **Endangered Species** (Work to protect these species, especially in your local area);
    - **Latchkey Program** (Provide valuable information to children who are forced to be latchkey kids to help them be safe);
    - **Literacy** (Help others improve their reading and writing skills in local schools or neighborhoods).

The list is endless if you can listen and think about our world.

Helping Sprouts Choose Their Own Justice Themes

When the Sprouts have become more familiar with the purpose and content of Justice Time, you will want to encourage them to participate in choosing new justice issues. Communication with one another will be a big factor in these decisions. Here are three practices that can help you to be successful in deciding on your justice topic.

- **First,** take a look at what is going on in the world around you. For instance, one group chose to promote peace in our world by earning money to purchase a Peace Pole at the Winter Olympic games in Salt Lake City. The project resulted in meaningful conversations about what peace is, what Sprouts can do locally to help achieve peace, and how

Sprouts can encourage others to participate in peace-building behavior. The self-discovery was amazing.

- **Second,** take a look at what is affecting your Sprouts. What are they talking about? What are they angry about? What do they have a passion for? Listening and asking these questions can help you determine a justice issue that your Sprouts can get excited about. For example, one group found that many in the group were being bullied at school, or they knew a close friend who was being bullied. This led to some great discussions on what they could do in different situations.

- **Third,** listen to what your Sprouts are not saying. What are the issues they are silently dealing with that may raise a red flag for you as adults? This listening may lead to a way to use Justice Time as a learning time. In one Sprouts group the leaders heard their fifth graders discuss their babysitting duties for their younger brothers and sisters. Immediately, discussions began to develop around the Sprouts' readiness to handle emergency situations and proper babysitting techniques. Babysitting became that group's justice issue. Not only did they learn about it, but then they planned a lock-in and each invited two or three friends who were also dealing with those same situations to learn about babysitting and managing emergencies. What they learned will make a difference for many babies and younger brothers and sisters.

Through these three practices there can be endless possibilities of discovery and learning. Pick one and see what develops.

Communicate With Bulletin Boards

Use bulletin boards or display boards to keep the whole congregation informed about what is going on with their children in the Sprouts group. The bulletin boards will keep the congregation in touch with the Sprouts, and they will help the congregation see what the children are doing as they become involved in justice issues. Display such things as
- photographs of Sprouts participants;
- a photo-journal of a Sprouts justice project;
- drawings from Sprouts activities;
- children's letters to government leaders or other results of justice projects;
- a world map that shows a part of the world that the children are learning about;
- information about a justice project.

Encourage the children to participate in creating the displays. They will benefit from the experience of being an active and valued part of their congregation's faith community.

Evaluate the Sessions

It is important for the success of the Sprouts ministry, as of any ministry, to evaluate regularly. Evaluation is the tool that will enable you to keep the program fresh and relevant for the children who participate.

- Each Sprouts leader needs to evaluate each individual session to make decisions about planning for the next session.

- It is also important for the entire leadership team to meet periodically for evaluation. They must evaluate the schedule, the sessions' content, and other details of the weekly meetings. Their evaluation will help determine what additional training and support leaders need.

- Sprouts children gain a sense of ownership when they are involved in ongoing evaluation. Give them opportunities to suggest topics for Justice Time, to plan ways to publicize upcoming terms of Sprouts, or to make reports to the congregation about the Sprouts ministry.

- Give parents an opportunity to evaluate too. Input from parents may be your best source of information about how Sprouts is affecting the lives of the children who participate.

In Pompano Beach, Florida, where Sprouts groups were first formed, Sprouts and their families were invited to a barbecue and swim party after the first two terms of Sprouts. The children and their parents were asked to complete an evaluation. Such feedback was invaluable, both because it confirmed that the Sprouts ministry is a significant ministry and because it allowed the originators of the program to make improvements from the beginning. You may want to plan a special time to insure that you get the evaluation information you need. (See sample evaluation forms for children, parents, and leaders on pages 73–75.)

Plan for the Future

- As you approach the end of each term, talk with the children about their participation in the next term.

- Begin publicity and registration for new and returning participants.

- Before the beginning of each new term, continue sending a letter to parents of potential Sprouts, inviting their children to participate in the new term.

- Meet with your leadership team to plan Justice Time sessions.

- Assign responsibilities for contacting guest speakers, arranging field trips, or other organizational jobs.

Endnote
1 From *Guide for Covenant Discipleship Groups,* by Gayle Turner Watson (Discipleship Resources, 2000), page 12. See also *The Book of Discipline—2000,* ¶ 1116.2a.

Sprouts Session-Planning Sheet

Planning Date: _____ Leadership: _____

Issues to Discuss: _____

Sprouts Meeting Date: _____ Time: _____ Location: _____

Covenant Time

Facilitator(s): _____

Issues: _____

_____

Room Setup: _____

Supplies: _____

_____

Justice Time

Theme: _____

Learning Activity	**Person Responsible**
1.	
2.	
3.	
4.	
5.	
6.	

Room Setup: _____

Supplies: _____

_____

Snack: _____ Person(s) Responsible: _____

Transportation Needs: _____

Next Planning Session Date: _____

Sample Sprouts Group Covenant

Preamble
We want to love God and our neighbors.
We want to witness to Jesus Christ in the world
through acts of kindness, justice, worship, and devotion, guided by the Holy Spirit.
We promise these things to God.
We know that God will forgive us when we make a mistake.
We will be faithful Sprouts.

Acts of Kindness
We will help a family member.
We will share.

Acts of Justice
We will be Ring Leaders for Ring Recycling.
We will learn about hunger and help hungry people.

Acts of Worship
We will attend worship at church each week, if possible.
We will attend Sunday school each week, if possible.

Acts of Devotion
We will pray daily.
We will read our Bibles.

Conclusion
We make this promise, trusting in God's grace to help us
love God and our neighbor in all that we do.

_____ _____ _____

_____ _____ _____

Signatures of Group Members

MY PERSONAL COVENANT

I will be a faithful member of my group as we encourage and support each other.

_____ _____

Signature   *Date*

Sprouts Group Covenant

Preamble

Acts of Kindness

Acts of Justice

Acts of Worship

Acts of Devotion

Conclusion

_____   _____   _____

_____   _____   _____

Signatures of Group Members

MY PERSONAL COVENANT

I will be a faithful member of my group as we encourage and support each other.

_____   _____

Signature   *Date*

Ritual for Covenanting

Opening Prayer: Dear Lord, thank you for the opportunities you give us each day. Thank you for the chance we have to share our faith and love with one another. Be with us today as we make this covenant with you and with our group. Help us be faithful to you as we live out this covenant. Amen.

Leader *(while lighting a candle on the worship table)*: Because this covenant is a promise between God and us as well as among us, and Christ is the light of the world, we light this candle as a sign of Christ's presence with us. As this candle burns, let us remember the importance of the symbol of light and our responsibility to be God's light in the world.

Group: Christ is present with us, and we are grateful. Come, Lord Jesus.

Leader: Let us read the opening lines of our covenant together:

Group *(replace with your group's preamble, if different)*:
We know that God loves us, no matter what.
We want to love God and our neighbors.
We want to witness to Jesus Christ in the world
through acts of kindness, justice, worship, and devotion,
guided by the Holy Spirit.
We promise these things to God.
We know that God will forgive us when we make a mistake.
With God's help, we will be faithful Sprouts.

Leader: The Bible tells us in the Old Testament in Jeremiah 31:33: "This is the covenant that I will make with the house of Israel after those days, says the LORD: I will put my law within them, and I will write it on their hearts; and I will be their God, and they shall be my people." Let us all take turns sharing the parts of our covenant with one another.

(Go around the circle, each taking a turn reading aloud one part of the group covenant. Continue reading in the circle until all the covenant has been read.)

Leader: As this is written on our hearts, let us bear witness to one another by signing our covenants together.

(Sign the covenants in silence.)

Closing Prayer: Dear Lord, be with us in the weeks ahead as we strive to be faithful to Jesus through this covenant. Please help each of us to be a faithful member of the group. Help us to take what is written on our hearts and see it through. Let us truly be your witnesses and your light in your world. Amen.

(Extinguish the candle.)

Sprouts

Journal

This journal belongs to

_____

→

Week of _____

LOVING NEIGHBORS

Acts of Kindness

Acts of Justice

Acts of Devotion

Acts of Worship

LOVING GOD

Prayer requests from my group:

My prayer concerns:

Date _____

      Theme:

_____

What does this Bible passage say to me?

_____

_____

_____

What questions do I have about this Bible passage?

_____

_____

_____

What does this Bible passage say about my life and how I should live?

_____

_____

_____

Prayer

_____

_____

_____

Sprouts Evaluation for Children

I was a Sprout in the Spring ____ Summer ____ Fall ____ Winter ____ *(check all that apply)* in the year(s) _____ .

What did you like about Sprouts? _____

_____

What would make Sprouts better? _____

_____

How many times a week did you usually read the Bible? *(Circle one.)*

1   2   3   4   5   6   7

What keeps you from reading the Bible? _____

_____

What could we do to help you read the Bible more? _____

_____

What difference has Sprouts made in your family life? _____

    School life? _____

    Relationship to friends? _____

    Church life? _____

How did you use your Sprouts journal?

____ wrote my own prayer requests   ____ wrote the group's prayer requests

____ wrote my Acts each week   ____ other _____

What changes in the journal would make it more useful for you? _____

_____

What did you like about Covenant Time in the Sprouts meetings? _____

What would you change about Covenant Time? _____

What did you like about Justice Time? _____

What would you change about Justice Time? _____

What issues would you like to learn about and work on as justice issues? _____

_____

Sprouts Evaluation for Parents

What most influenced your child's decision to participate in Sprouts?
(Rank from 1 to 5, 1 being most influential and 5 being least influential.)

_____ Parent
_____ Adult leader
_____ Friend
_____ Publicity
_____ Purpose of Sprouts
_____ Other:_____

Did your child talk to you about Sprouts?_____

What did he or she say? _____

_____

How often did you remind your child to do the following activities?
Often (O); Sometimes (S); Never (N)

_____ Pray
_____ Read the Bible
_____ Write in the Sprouts journal

How many times a week did your child usually do the following activities?
_____ Read the Bible
_____ Pray

What keeps your child from reading the Bible?

What could the church do to help your child read the Bible?

What difference has Sprouts made in your family life?

    In your child's school life?

    In your child's relationship to friends?

    In your child's relationship to church?

    In the life of the church?

What improvements would you suggest for Sprouts?

Sprouts Evaluation for Leaders

I served as a leader for Covenant Time _____ for Justice Time _____

Describe how you saw Sprouts influencing the life of the children in your Sprouts group. (Do not mention anyone by name.)

_____

_____

_____

How did you and your Sprouts use the Sprouts journal? _____

_____

What changes in the format of the journal would have made it more useful in your group?

_____

_____

What improvements would you suggest for training Sprouts leaders?

_____

_____

What improvements would you suggest for Covenant Time?

_____

_____

What improvements would you suggest for Justice Time?

_____

_____

What issues can you suggest as possibilities for justice themes for future Sprouts groups?

_____

_____

What difference has being a Sprouts leader made in your own spiritual faith and growth?

_____

_____

Are you a member of an adult Covenant Discipleship group? _____

Would you be interested in being a member of an adult Covenant Discipleship group?_____

Part 5

Sprouts

Worship Resources and Activity Ideas

Other seeds fell on good soil and
brought forth grain, some a hundredfold,
some sixty, some thirty.
Matthew 13:8

Worship Resources for Sprouts Groups

Christian disciples are shaped by worship and prayer as well as by reading the Bible and taking part in the sacraments of baptism and Holy Communion. This understanding and confidence supports the prayers offered here for the use of Sprouts and their congregations.

A historical practice among Christians is to affirm one another in prayer and bless one another for prayer by a simple responsory: "The Lord be with you" and the reply of the group, "And also with you." The prayers provided here offer this mutual empowerment as a way to begin prayer together.

Opening Prayer
Leader: The Lord is with you.
Sprouts: And also with you.
All: Jesus, you said that whenever two or three were together, you would be among us. So, thank you for being here with us as we share our acts of kindness, justice, worship, and devotion and grow in faithfulness to you. Amen.

Closing Prayer
Leader: The Lord is with you.
Sprouts: And also with you.
All: Breath of God, wind that makes all winds blow, fill us with your life and send us out to love you and our neighbors, especially the poor, the hurting, and the unloved, in the name of Jesus. Amen.

Prayer of Thanksgiving[1]
Leader: The Lord is with you.
Sprouts: And also with you.
All: God of power and mercy,
   we thank you for all things that mirror your creating and saving love.
   We thank you for all of the blessings of this life.
   Above all we thank you
       for your saving and liberating work in Jesus Christ,
       for the means of grace, and
       for the hope of eternal life.
   Make us so aware of your kindness to us
       that our hearts may be always thankful,
       and that we may praise you,
   not only with our lips, but in our lives,
   by giving up ourselves to your service, and
   by walking before you in love and faithfulness all of our days.
   Amen.

Prayer of Confession and Forgiveness/Assurance[2]
Leader: The Lord is with you.
Sprouts: And also with you.
Leader: Let us confess our sin against God and our neighbor. *(Invite all to*

reflect silently on where their thoughts, words, and actions have been contrary to the way of love and justice.)

All: Merciful God,
we confess that we have sinned against you
by thought, word, and deed,
by what we have done and
by what we have left undone.
We have not loved you with our whole heart;
we have not loved our neighbors as ourselves.
We are truly sorry and we humbly repent.
Have mercy on us and forgive us
through your Son, Jesus Christ,
that we may rejoice in your will, and
walk in your ways,
to the glory of your name. Amen.

Leader: Hear the good news: When Jesus told of the joy of the woman who found the coin she had lost and invited her neighbors to party with her, Jesus said, "I tell you, there is joy in the presence of the angels of God over one sinner who repents." In the name of Jesus Christ, you are found and forgiven.

Group to Leader: In the name of Jesus Christ, you are found and forgiven.

All: Glory to God! Amen.

Prayers From *The United Methodist Hymnal*

76	Trinity Sunday	403	For True Life
201	Advent	412	Prayer of John Chrysostom
231	Christmas	423	Finding Rest in God
253	Baptism of the Lord	429	For Our Country
255	Epiphany	446	Serving the Poor
268	Lent	456	For Courage to Do Justice
281	Passion/Palm Sunday	457	For the Sick
283	Holy Thursday	461	For Those Who Mourn
284	Good Friday	466	An Invitation to Christ
320	Easter Vigil or Day	481	The Prayer of Saint Francis
321	Sundays of Easter	489	For God's Gifts
323	The Ascension	493	Three Things We Pray
329	Prayer to the Holy Spirit	495	The Sufficiency of God
335	An Invitation to the Holy Spirit	602	Concerning the Scriptures
353	Ash Wednesday	639	Bread and Justice
392	Prayer for a New Heart	689	At the Close of Day
401	For Holiness of Heart	721	Christ the King

1 This prayer is based on the General Thanksgiving in *The United Methodist Book of Worship* (550) and in The Book of Common Prayer (in the section "Evening Prayer").

2 Based on a prayer of confession from The Book of Common Prayer, 1979.

A Wesleyan Covenant Prayer

Note to leaders and Sprouts: There is wisdom and power in the language of the traditional prayer. While the contemporary translation is easier to understand, the traditional prayer has a special power and connection to the generations that have lived and prayed it before us. Groups that use this prayer frequently will learn to appreciate its language and force in shaping their discipleship.

The historic and traditional text

I am no longer my own, but thine.
Put me to what thou wilt, rank me with
  whom thou wilt.
Put me to doing, put me to suffering.
Let me be employed by thee or laid aside
  for thee, exalted for thee or brought low
  for thee.
Let me be full, let me be empty.
Let me have all things, let me have nothing.
I freely and heartily yield all things to thy
  pleasure and disposal.
And now, O glorious and blessed God,
  Father, Son, and Holy Spirit,
thou art mine, and I am thine. So be it.
And the covenant which I have made on
  earth, let it be ratified in heaven.
Amen.

A contemporary American version

God, I offer myself to you, even when I want
  to belong to myself.
Put me in the places you want me to be.
Place me next to the people you want me to
  love and serve.
Choose what you want me to do.
Let me be busy or let me rest as you decide
  for me.
Let me have plenty or let me have little.
By a willing choice,
I give the cares and details of my life to you.
Now, glorious and always present God, you
  are mine and I am yours.
By the power of your Spirit working in me,
  may I always keep the covenant I have
  made with you.
Amen.

Love Feast for Use With Children

The United Methodist Book of Worship contains historical information, suggestions for the use of the Love Feast, appropriate hymns and Scriptures, as well as the service itself (pages 581–84). Given the time constraints of the Sprouts meeting, it is impossible to use a full service. What follows is an abbreviated order, which preserves the form of the *Book of Worship* service but allows children to experience the Love Feast.

Since some children may see similarities between the Love Feast and Holy Communion, it is important to make clear to the Sprouts that this is not the sacrament of Holy Communion at which an ordained elder presides. Instead, it is a simple sharing of food led by a layperson.

The Sprouts may include the reading of their group Covenant within the Love Feast, followed by each Sprout in turn telling her or his Acts of Kindness, Justice, Worship, and Devotion. The reading of the Covenant and each Sprout's time of accountability would replace the "Address or Personal Witness to the Scripture" and the "Testimonies, Prayers, and Singing" portions of the Love Feast in the *Book of Worship*.

Brief Order for a Love Feast

Hymn (Tune: TERRA BEATA [144] or DIADEMATA [327], *The United Methodist Hymnal*)

Father of earth and heaven,
>Thy hungry children feed,
Thy grace be to our spirits given,
>That true immortal bread.
Grant us and all our race
>In Jesus Christ to prove
The sweetness of thy pardoning grace,
>The manna of thy love.
>>(Charles Wesley)

Scripture

Prayer

Loving God,
We thank you for your abundant grace.
We give thanks that you teach us to love one another.
We rejoice in the beginnings of your loving life that we feel in our hearts.
We have tasted the comfort of your love in the fellowship of the Spirit;
This makes us sensitive to the needs of others.

We sincerely desire that your love come to completion in us
>so that more and more the smallness of our spirits
>>may change to a larger and larger outlook on all human beings.
Especially empower us with eager love as we have been loved by you.
We want to love our brothers and sisters and show your love
>through our lives in your world. Amen.

Our Covenant

(Group reads its covenant together. Each person gives a personal account of discipleship.)

Lord's Prayer

Fellowship of Eating and Passing the Cup

As the children pass food and drink, they say:
"God loves you, and there is nothing you can do about it."

Hymn or Doxology

Dismissal

Go forth to love God and your neighbor in all that you do.
Go to live as witnesses to Jesus Christ in the world and to follow his teachings through acts
>of kindness, justice, worship, and devotion, under the guidance of the Holy Spirit.
In the name of God—Father, Son, and Holy Spirit,
Go in peace to bear the light of God's love to the world. Amen.

Sources: *The United Methodist Book of Worship; The United Methodist Hymnal;* and *Methodism and the Love-Feast,* by Frank Baker (New York: Macmillan, 1957).

Suggested Scriptures for the Love Feast

Psalm 145:8-21   *1 John 4:7-21*   *Luke 14:16-24*
1 Corinthians 13   *Matthew 22:34-40*   *John 6:25-35*
2 Corinthians 9:6-15 *Luke 9:12-17*   *John 15:1-17*
Philippians 2:5-11   *Luke 10:25-37*

Suggested Hymns for the Love Feast

The United Methodist Hymnal

94	Praise God, From Whom All Blessings Flow
186	Alleluia
389	Freely, Freely
402	Lord, I Want to Be a Christian
422	Jesus, Thine All-Victorious Love
432	Jesu, Jesu
560	Help Us Accept Each Other
566	Blest Be the Dear Uniting Love
572	Pass It On
583	Sois la Semilla
659	Jesus Our Friend and Brother
665	Go Now in Peace

The Faith We Sing

2040	Awesome God
2167	More Like You
2168	Love the Lord Your God
2171	Make Me a Channel of Your Peace
2175	Together We Serve
2176	Make Me a Servant
2179	Live in Charity
2222	The Servant Song
2223	They'll Know We Are Christians by Our Love
2224	Make Us One
2226	Bind Us Together
2233	Where Children Belong

Suggested Songs and Hymns for Use With Children

From *The Faith We Sing*

2013	Bless the Lord
2014	Alleluia
2017	Come, Rejoice in God
2021	What a Mighty God We Serve
2026	Halle, Halle, Halleluja
2028	Clap Your Hands
2054	Nothing Can Trouble
2057	Be Still and Know That I Am God
2072	Amen, Amen
2130	The Summons
2150	Lord, Be Glorified
2156	Give Peace
2157	Come and Fill Our Hearts

2166	Christ Beside Me
2168	Love the Lord Your God
2176	Make Me a Servant
2179	Live in Charity
2193	Lord, Listen to Your Children Praying
2195	In the Lord I'll Be Ever Thankful
2200	O Lord, Hear My Prayer
2214	Lead Me, Guide Me
2219	Goodness Is Stronger Than Evil
2236	Gather Us In
2278	The Lord's Prayer
2280	The Lord Bless and Keep You

From *The United Methodist Hymnal*

Possible Activities for Sprouts Groups

General Activities

- **Sprouts Newsletter**—Send a Sprouts newsletter to parents periodically to keep them informed of what is going on in Sprouts.

- **Family Social**—Have a family social at the beginning or the end of a Sprouts term.

- **Acrostics**—Each letter can be part of a phrase or just a word that relates to Sprouts or discipleship. SPROUTS becomes Spirit-filled People Recruiting Others Under the Spirit. Use words such as Kindness, Prayer, your church name, or even children's names.

- **Games**—Use popular game formats (Jeopardy, Wheel of Fortune, Who Wants to Be a Millionaire?) to create your own learning games.

- **Snack Sharing**—Create a snack box (a large plastic container). Let everyone take turns bringing the snack—whoever is assigned to bring snacks next time can take the box home and return with it full of snacks, and then it can go home with the next person.

- **Make Sprouts T-shirts**—T-shirts can be a visible sign to the congregation that something is happening in Sprouts. The front of the shirt can include the name Sprouts and some kind of symbol, such as the Jerusalem cross. The Sprouts can decorate the back of the shirts with words or pictures that represent faith or responses to justice themes. One group put WWSD— What Would Sprouts Do?

- **Junior Counselors**—Invite fifth and sixth graders who have already been through Sprouts to be part of a younger Sprouts group as Junior Counselors. They can function as group leaders alongside the adult Covenant Time leaders.

- **Relate Sprouts to Older Generations**—Children need to be in relationships with older adults. Sprouts can interview older members of the congregation to find out how they are involved in volunteer ministry. Encourage the older adults to help the children understand how being in mission has helped them to grow as Christian disciples.

- **Tell Others About Sprouts**—As one group did, offer to staff a booth about Sprouts at the meeting of your annual conference. Arrange for the Sprouts to be there for a day, wearing their T-shirts.

- **Recognize Sprouts**—Plan a dedication service for Sprouts and Sprouts leaders before the sessions begin. After the sessions are over, ask Sprouts to wear their T-shirts to worship, where they will be recognized for the projects they have completed and for their growth in Christian discipleship.

- **Create a Ritual for Closing Each Session**—The format of the closing will be something that has meaning for the individual group.

- **Keep a Record of Your Covenant Keeping**—Use the clauses of the group covenant and the meeting dates of your group to create a grid to check off when Acts have been done to keep the various parts of the covenant.

Journal Activities

- **Encourage Spiritual Journaling**—Take the kids into the sanctuary or a chapel. Dim the lights slightly (do not make it hard to read the journal!), play meditative music, and let the children spend some time writing to God in their journals.

- **Journal in Response to Bible Verses**—Give each Sprout a page with a Bible verse at the top. Suggest specific questions or thoughts as topics for journaling. Provide space for writing or for drawing. During Covenant Time talk about the responses.

Kindness Activities

- **Visit a Nursing Home**—Go to a nursing home and help with an activity with residents there like making a craft, visiting, or singing to them.

- **Make Christmas Ornaments**—Make Christmas ornaments for a family that does not have ornaments or the money to buy them.

- **Create an Ongoing "Chain of Kindness"**—Write each completed Act of Kindness on a paper link and add the links in a chain as a visible reminder of the children's fulfillment of their covenant. As the chain grows, drape it around the Sprouts meeting room.

- **Serve People Who Have No Homes**—Help prepare and serve meals for the guests at a nearby service agency. Plan ways for the children to interact with those they are serving.

- **Help an Afterschool/Childcare Program**—Provide a meal. Donate birthday boxes for an afterschool program for children in need. Donate clean toys to a facility that includes childcare.

- **Provide Food and Clothes**—Sponsor a collection of socks and underwear for a shelter for homeless people. Sponsor a food drive for a food bank.

- **Collect and Give Socks to Prisoners**—Include a spiritually uplifting card in each gift.

- **Crop Walk**—If your congregation already participates in Church World Service's Crop Walk, participate as a Sprouts group. If your congregation does not participate, help them get it started in your community.

- **Support Your Church's Staff**—Do yard work at the parsonage or find another way to support your pastor and other staff.

- **Choose an Environmental Project**—Adopt a section of road to maintain. Help out with a local environmental project.

- **Earn Money for a Mission Project**—Have a money-raising project for UMCOR (United Methodist Committee on Relief) or for another church-sponsored project. If there is a project in your own conference, plan a visit or even a day to help with the project.

- **Say Thank You**—Make cookies and brownies or thank-you cards for local police officers, firefighters, or staff members at a local service organization.

- **The Bishops' Initiative on Children and Poverty**—Get involved in whatever is happening in your church, district, or conference. If nothing is planned already, begin a churchwide program.

- **Collect Children's Books**—Donate them to a shelter for women and children or to families in a low-income area where children do not have adequate access to books.

Justice Activities

- **Extra Time for Justice Projects**—Take an afternoon and complete a justice project separate from your normal meeting time.

- **Cooperate With Other Groups**—Help your church become aware of local justice issues such as hunger or homelessness. Learn about and encourage your church to explore and consider involvement in such ministries as Interfaith Hospitality Network (churches that help house homeless families; visit www.nihn.org), Habitat for Humanity, or other helpful organizations.

- **Fun Activities**—Use videos as tools for spreading the word on your justice issue. Start an e-mail awareness chain. Use computers to create brochures or other informational items. Have a scavenger hunt to learn about your justice issue—make up clues that will send Sprouts gathering information all around your meeting space. They love doing this and it is active.

- **Prayer Vigils and Worship Services**—Sponsor prayer vigils or worship services relating to particular justice issues such as World AIDS Day.

- **Literacy Issues**—Learn about literacy and illiteracy. Perhaps older Sprouts can work with a school to tutor younger children. Sprouts can urge their congregation to begin a tutoring program.

- **Peacemakers**—Use the theme "Peacemakers: Build a New World," based on Matthew 5:9. Discuss articles relating to war and peace clipped from news magazines or newspapers. Learn about famous peacemakers. Have Sprouts sing "Let There Be Peace on Earth" in Sunday worship. Create "Build a New World" T-shirts.

- **Peace Pole**—Place a Peace Pole at church. Be sure to include education about the Pole and activities for the entire church. (For information on the Pole and how to buy one, see www.worldpeace.org/peacepoles.html.)

- **Peace Calendar**—Create a peace calendar. Let the Sprouts draw pictures of ways to bring peace to the world for each month on the calendar. Sell the calendars and give the money to a peace organization or to a local charity.

- **Violence Prevention**—Work with a local school on violence prevention programs. Sponsor a "Stop the Gun Violence" march from the church to a site about a mile away. On the vacant lot or other place, erect a cross representing each individual who was a victim of gun violence in your community during the past year. Invite media coverage.

- **Write Letters**—Write to legislators, local newspapers, manufacturers or businesses, church officials, or anyone who might have influence or power relating to the particular justice issue you are working on.

- **Make a Peace Banner or Quilt**—Each child can design his or her own panel, cut out appliqués of felt or fabric, or draw a design. Attach the small panels to the banner. Present the banner to the congregation at a Sunday worship service, perhaps on Peace with Justice Sunday.

- **Recycle**—Sponsor a recycling project of the plastic rings from aluminum-can packs so they can be recycled into new rings. (ITW Hi-Cone's Ring Leader Recycling Program provides free educational information, lesson plans, posters, and postage labels to pay for sending them the rings. See page 96 for contact information.)

- **Alternative Giving**—Educate your congregation about alternative forms of giving, such as donating to a charity in honor of someone rather than giving that person a gift, or buying gifts from programs like SERRV (phone 800-422-5915 or www.serrv.org/catalog/index.html) or Ten Thousand Villages (phone 717-859-8100 or www.villages.ca), which buy crafts and products at a fair price from artisans in developing countries. Sponsor a Heifer Project fair at church (see page 96).

- **Appreciate Differences**—Make a mural or banner entitled "All Belong: Appreciate Differences." Among the images include people of different colors, nationalities, religions, handicapping conditions, ages, economic conditions, or other categories.

- **Visit Other Churches**—Visit a nearby synagogue, a mosque, or a church of another Christian denomination. Invite children or families from that group to visit your church for a time of fellowship and mutual learning.

- **Visit an Ethnic Restaurant**—If you are working on peacemaking or inclusivity in Justice Time, consider a visit (perhaps with parents) to an ethnic restaurant most of your children are not familiar with (Greek, Lebanese, Guatemalan, and so forth).

- **Spend a Night in a Box**—After studying about homelessness, do what some Sprouts have done and spend a night sleeping in cardboard boxes, wearing only a T-shirt, shoes, and pants. Ask your congregation to provide you with food, money, blankets, and clothing that can later be given to a local shelter. You may even want to advertise in a local paper and invite others to contribute to the mission project.

Worship Activities
- **Holy Communion**—Study the background and meaning of Holy Communion. Then volunteer to help prepare the elements for a Communion service and/or to assist the pastor in serving Communion.

- **Communion Service**—Attend a Communion service together as a group.

- **Baptism**—Invite your pastor to teach about baptism. Arrange to have Sprouts come up front to have a better view or even to help during the next baptism service.

- **Learn About the Worship Service**—Help the children understand some of the forms and rituals of our worship service.

- **Volunteer**—Sprouts can volunteer as a group to hand out bulletins or to usher at a worship service.

Devotion Activities
- **Prayer Requests**—As the Sprouts enter the room each week, let them write their prayer concerns on a "Prayer Requests" list. (With younger groups, let an adult listen to the prayer requests and write them down.) Type up and then photocopy the list in time for the Sprouts to put it in their journals to use during the coming week.

- **Prayer Chain**—If your church has an active prayer chain, find a way for the Sprouts to be a part of it. Or start your own Sprouts prayer chain letting others in the church know that Sprouts will pray for their needs.

- **ACTS**—Teach the prayer acronym *ACTS: A*doration, *C*onfession, *T*hanksgiving, *S*upplication. Create a group prayer together each week, using this formula.

- **Write a Prayer Book**—Provide copies of the prayer book to put in the pews so that people can use them as they prepare for worship.

- **Use *Pockets* Magazine**—Give special attention to "Pocketsful of Prayer."

- **Sentence Prayers**—Teach children one-sentence prayers that are easily memorized, such as "Create in me a clean heart, O God" (Psalm 51:10).

- **Make a Time Capsule**—Let the children put their written prayer requests inside an empty bottle and then bury it, as one Sprouts group has done. After eight weeks, dig up the bottle, read the prayer requests, and discuss how God has answered prayers.

- **Images of God**—Help the children choose a name or image for God that reflects some aspect of God's love and care for us (captain, creator, father, mother hen, or grandmother).

- **When God Says No**—Discuss what it means when "No" is an answer to prayer. Help the children consider how they should respond to the many possibilities for God's answers to prayer.

- **Assign Prayer Partners**—Prayer partners can be children within the Sprouts group or could be adults, youth, or former Sprouts.

- **Use the Children's Prayer Calendar**—Send a birthday card to a missionary or to a child of a missionary listed in the calendar. Encourage the children to pray for missionaries every day. (The Children's Prayer Calendar is available from the General Board of Global Ministries; see page 96 for contact information.)

- **Use *Pockets* Magazine**—Give special attention to "Pocketsful of Scripture." Read the Scripture in class and discuss any questions or insights the children may have.

- **Use Your Own Words**—Have the Sprouts rewrite a Bible passage or story in modern-day language. Let them make a video or perform it as a drama for a younger audience. Encourage the Sprouts to talk about what the story or passage means to them.

- **Luke 4:16-30**—Compare Martin Luther King Jr.'s dream of equality and justice to Jesus' proclamation of Isaiah's text on justice when he preached in his hometown synagogue.

- **Hunger and Poverty Issues**—Use some of these passages for study during Covenant Time: 1 Kings 17:1-16 (Elijah and the widow); Luke 16:19-31 (Lazarus and the rich man); James 2:14-17 (actions speak louder than words).

- **Nature**—Take the Sprouts outside in nature settings. Encourage them to write about nature—nature poems or observations of nature as an expression of God's creative power. During Covenant Time ask each child to tell about a special nature observation she or he made during the week.

- **Create a Devotional Book**—Ask youth or adults whom the Sprouts admire to write a Lenten or Advent "message of hope." Add the messages to the children's own devotional writings. Publish a booklet to distribute or to sell to raise money for a mission project. Be sure that you get written permission from each writer before distributing or selling the booklet!

Part
6

Sprouts

Resources for Additional Planning

The faithful will abound
with blessings.
Proverbs 28:20

Resources published by Discipleship Resources may be ordered online at www.discipleshipresources.org; by phone at 800-685-4370; by fax at 770-442-9742; or by mail from Discipleship Resources Distribution Center, PO Box 1616, Alpharetta, GA 30009-1616.

Contact information for many of the other resource providers mentioned here can be found on the Agencies and Organizations page (page 96).

Covenant Discipleship Resources

The Sprouts Network—www.sproutsnet.org. Log on for more information about Covenant Discipleship with children. You can ask questions, find additional resources for use with your group, or catch up on the latest ideas from other leaders of Sprouts groups.

Accountable Discipleship: Living in God's Household, by Steven W. Manskar (Discipleship Resources, 2000).

Covenant Discipleship Quarterly. Send your name and address to Covenant Discipleship Quarterly, PO Box 340003, Nashville, TN 37203-0003 or register at www.sproutsnet.org to receive this quarterly newsletter about Covenant Discipleship ministry, including a special section about Sprouts.

Guide for Class Leaders: A Model for Christian Formation, by Grace Bradford (Discipleship Resources, 1999).

Guide for Covenant Discipleship Groups, by Gayle Turner Watson (Discipleship Resources, 2000).

Sprouts: Covenant Discipleship With Children, by Edie Genung Harris and Shirley L. Ramsey (Discipleship Resources, 2002).

Together in Love: Covenant Discipleship With Youth, by David C. Sutherland (Discipleship Resources, 1999).

Resources for Justice Themes

Animal Crackers: World Hunger Education for Children, Youth, and Adults (Heifer Project International, 1999). A free educational resource from the Heifer Project.

Christian Social Action, a bimonthly journal published by the General Board of Church and Society.

Crop Walk resources. Materials on hunger education are published in connection with Church World Service's Crop Walk (888-297-2767; www.churchworldservice.org/resrcsht), some of which are useful with children.

Educating for Peace and Justice: Religious Dimensions, K–6, by James McGinnis (Institute for Peace and Justice, 1993).

Educators for Social Responsibility. 23 Garden Street, Cambridge, MA 02138. 800-370-2515. www.esrnational.org. Offers a catalog of resources on topics related to justice.

Elementary Perspectives 1: Teaching Concepts of Peace and Conflict, by William J. Kreidler (Educators for Social Responsibility, 1990).

Fifty Simple Things Kids Can Do to Save the Earth, by The Earthworks Group (Andrews and McMeel, 1990).

Finding Solutions to Hunger: Kids Can Make a Difference, by Stephanie Kempf (World Hunger Year, 1997). A teacher's guide with twenty-five lessons for children to learn about and respond to hunger. To order, visit the Kids Can Make a Difference website (www.kids@kids.maine.org) or call 207-439-9588.

Gifts That Make a Difference: How to Buy Hundreds of Great Gifts Sold Through Nonprofits, by Ellen Berry (Foxglove Publishing, 1992). Cross-referenced by group, interest, and kind of gift. Includes ideas for alternative giving (such as buying an acre of rainforest).

Great Mission Ideas for Workers With Children, by Faye Wilson-Beach (General Board of Global Missions, no date). Excellent ideas for teaching the biblical basis of mission and educating about mission. Includes suggestions for child-oriented service projects.

The Kid's Guide to Social Action: How to Solve the Social Problems You Choose—and Turn Creative Thinking Into Positive Action, by Barbara A. Lewis (Free Spirit Publishing, 1998). Includes suggestions for choosing a justice issue and for doing justice projects. Includes examples of kids who got things done.

Mission Means. A monthly packet of mission-education ideas produced by the General Board of Global Ministries.

Peacemaking Creatively Through the Arts: A Handbook of Educational Activities and Experiences for Children, by Phyllis Vos Wezeman (Educational Ministries, 1990).

Peace With Justice Newsletter, free to members of the Peace With Justice Program of the General Board of Church and Society. Join by phone or at their website (see page 96).

Teaching Kids to Care and Share: 300+ Mission and Service Ideas for Children, by Jolene L. Roehlkepartain (Abingdon Press, 2000).

Teaching Tolerance. A magazine, free to educators, published twice a year by the Southern Poverty Law Center (400 Washington Avenue, Montgomery, AL 36104 or www.tolerance.org/teach).

What on Earth Can You Do? Making Your Church a Creation Awareness Center, by Donna Lehman (Herald Press, 1993). For adults (and youth), but has lots of good examples that Sprouts leaders can adapt for their groups.

Resources for Worship

A Child Shall Lead: Children in Worship (A Sourcebook for Christian Educators, Musicians, and Clergy), edited by John Witvliet (Choristers Guild, 1999). Helps for teaching children about worship and for involving children in worship. Includes a resource list. (Contact the Choristers Guild at 972-271-1521; fax 972-840-3113; or www.choristersguild.org.)

Forbid Them Not: Involving Children in Sunday Worship, by Carolyn Brown (Abingdon Press, 1992–1994). Helps for using the readings of the Revised

Common Lectionary with children. There are volumes for years A, B, and C. An index includes the readings for all three lectionary years.

Resources for Children

A Country Far Away, by Nigel Gray (Orchard Books, 1989). Children's book with one text and parallel illustrations of a child's life in Africa and a child's life in the United States. Great for looking at differences and similarities between cultures and at the universality of humanity.

Sadako and the Thousand Paper Cranes, by Eleanor Coerr (Dell Publishing, 1977).The story of a Japanese girl who is stricken with leukemia after the bombing of Hiroshima. A legend says that if she folds a thousand paper cranes, she will be well again.

Resources for Devotion

Children and Prayer: A Shared Pilgrimage, by Betty Shannon Cloyd (Upper Room, 1997).

Children's Prayer Calendar. Lists the names and birth dates of United Methodist missionaries. Produced by the General Board of Global Ministries (see page 96).

Hey, God, Let's Talk! (Abingdon Press, 2000). Six lessons to teach children about prayer. Includes a music CD and reproducible pages for each lesson.

In God's Name, by Sandy Eisenberg Sasso (Jewish Lights Publishing, 1994).

Pockets. A magazine for ages 6–12 from The Upper Room. Includes puzzles, games, stories, poems, Scripture, and prayers to help children grow closer to God.

Resources for Leaders

Capture the Moment: Building Faith Traditions for Families, by Rick and Sue Isbell (Discipleship Resources, 1998). Describes the significance of twenty-six key milestones in a family's life together. Includes Bible references and ideas for celebrating the events. Includes a leader's guide.

Growing Compassionate Kids: Helping Kids See Beyond Their Backyard, by Jan Johnson (Upper Room, 2001). Although written for parents, this book includes lots of good ideas that can be adapted for Sprouts groups.

How Do Our Children Grow? Introducing Children to God, Jesus, the Bible, Prayer, Church, by Delia Halverson (Chalice Press, 1999). Although written for parents, contains many good ideas.

Keeping in Touch: Christian Formation and Teaching, by Carol F. Krau (Discipleship Resources, 1999). Focuses on helping teachers discover what they need to create environments for nurturing people toward Christian discipleship.

Out of the Basement: A Holistic Approach to Children's Ministry, by Diane C. Olson (Discipleship Resources, 2001). Helps local church leaders examine their ministry with children to discover a vision that recognizes children as growing disciples of Jesus Christ.

Praying in the Wesleyan Spirit: 52 Prayers for Today, by Paul Chilcote (Upper Room, 2001). Fifty-two of Wesley's standard sermons transposed into devotional prayers. Contemporary language, yet faithful to Wesley's message. A Scripture reference and a Charles Wesley hymn accompany each prayer.

Praying With John Wesley, by David A. de Silva (Discipleship Resources, 2001). An updated interpretation of Wesley's prayers by twenty-first-century Christians. Takes the reader through one full week of morning and evening devotions based on the model for daily prayer developed by John Wesley.

Safe Sanctuaries: Reducing the Risk of Child Abuse in the Church, by Joy Thornburg Melton (Discipleship Resources, 1998). Outlines policies and procedures to prevent child abuse. Includes ideas for training, forms, and a sample worship service.

Side by Side: Families Learning and Living the Faith Together, by Delia Halverson (Abingdon Press, 2002).

Agencies and Organizations

Office of Accountable Discipleship
General Board of Discipleship
PO Box 340003
Nashville, TN 37203-0003

Discipleship Resources
PO Box 340003
Nashville, TN 37203-0003
www.discipleshipresources.org
800-685-4370

The Upper Room
PO Box 340003
Nashville, TN 37203-0003
www.upperroom.org
800-972-0433

Cokesbury
201 Eighth Avenue, South
Nashville, TN 37202
www.cokesbury.com
800-672-1789

General Board of Church and Society
100 Maryland Avenue, NE
Washington, DC 20002-5664
www.umc-gbcs.org
202-488-5600

General Board of Global Ministries
Service Center
7820 Reading Road, Caller No. 1800
Cincinnati, OH 45222-1800
www.gbgm-umc.org/
800-305-9857 or Fax 513-761-3722

United Methodist Committee on Relief (UMCOR)
World Hunger/Poverty Program
Room #330
475 Riverside Drive
New York, NY 10115
www.gbgm-umc.org/umcor/
212-870-3816

ALTERNATIVES for Simple Living
PO Box 2787
Sioux City, IA 51106
800-821-6153 or Fax 712-274-1402
www.simpleliving.org

Bread for the World
50 F Street NW, Suite 500
Washington, DC 20001
www.bread.org
800-822-7323 or Fax 202-639-9401

Children's Defense Fund
25 E Street, NW
Washington, DC 20001
www.childrensdefense.org
202-628-8787

Church World Service
PO Box 968
Elkhart, IN 46515
www.churchworldservice.org
800-297-1516 or Fax 574-262-0966

ECHO (Educational Concerns for Hunger Organization)
17391 Durrance Road
North Ft. Myers, FL 33917
www.echonet.org
239-543-3246 or Fax 239-543-5317

Heifer Project International
PO Box 8058
Little Rock, AR 72203
www.heifer.org
800-422-0474

Institute for Peace and Justice
4144 Lindell Boulevard, #408
St. Louis, MO 63108
www.ipj-ppj.org
314-533-4445 or Fax 314-715-6455

ITW Hi-Cone (Recycling Plastic Rings)
1140 West Bryn Mawr Avenue
Itasca, IL 60143
www.ringleader.com/quest/menu/index.html
630-773-9300 or Fax 630-773-3015

Presbyterian Peacemaking Program
100 Witherspoon Street
Louisville, KY 40202
www.horeb.pcusa.org/peacemaking
800-524-2612

Trees for Life
3006 W. St. Louis
Wichita, KS 67203
www.treesforlife.org
316-945-6929